MUST KILL TV

By Ken Levine

Story by Ken Levine & David Isaacs

MUST KILL TV

CHAPTER 1

BLEEP!

Charles Muncie had a text message, as he did every morning at exactly five o'clock.

He rolled over in bed, causing his wife, Sondra, to stir but not wake up. He snatched the phone off the night table, checked the message, and screamed. This woke Sondra up.

"What? What?" she said, panicked.

"Goddamn Honey Boo Boo! I want to run that bitch over with my car!"

"Oh, for crissakes! Not again!"

"Did I wake you?"

"Did you wake me? What the fuck?!"

"I'm sorry."

"You wake me every goddamn day!"

Prior to the text message, you would have thought Charles and Sondra Muncie were the perfect settled married couple. Lying in bed, entwined together. Both were in their late thirties. Charles had butterscotch locks and steel-blue eyes and was still one waist size away from danger. Sondra was tall, statuesque, with long dark hair cascading over her shoulders. Very wholesome looking, which for Southern California meant no major work done. They lived in Brentwood, a very upscale section of West Los Angeles, in a stunning two-story white home that was of traditional Cape Cod design—so it fit right in with the craftsman house, the all-glass monstrosity, and the Persian palace that shared the block. They had one child—an eight-year-old daughter, Kelly Rose, who was as precious as that name.

"I'm sorry. I am," Charles said, "but our entire lineup last night got obliterated by the Honey Boo Boo special on NBC. It's one thing to play to the lowest common denominator, but this is like programming to mollusks. I'd bring back *Hee Haw*, but I'm afraid that's still too highbrow for them."

Sondra sat up in bed. "I can't stand this."

Charles took a deep breath. "I know. You're right. Allow me a moment to regain my serenity." He closed his eyes and repeated his mantra. "I am the president of ABN. We are okay because I am okay. I set the tone. I create the atmosphere. *A leader is a dealer in hope.*"

He let that internalize for a moment, opened his eyes, and said, "Okay. Let's get some sleep."

"No, no, no, no, no." Before he could roll over, she tugged at his shoulder. "Charles. I'm serious. I've been giving this a lot of thought—a *lot* of thought, and I think we would be better off in separate bedrooms."

"What?" This caught him completely by surprise.

"You're up half the night, which keeps me up, and then when I fall asleep, you scream and scare the shit out of me."

"But I have to see the overnights. It's my job. Michelle Obama doesn't kick her husband out. And he gets woken up with nuclear threats."

"You're the president of a television network. There's a slight difference."

"Right. When he's in a crisis he can lower interest rates or invade Korea. It's not like I can throw Honey Boo Boo in Guantanamo."

Sondra folded her arms and just glared at him.

"Okay," he conceded, "no more screaming when I see the numbers. Promise."

"It used to just be once a week."

"Yes, but that was when we were number one in all age-groups across the board."

"Then twice a week, and now it's up to four."

Charles buried his head in his hands. His management style was to always give the impression that all was well. And since perception in Hollywood is often more important than reality, that executive approach had served him well. But playing it close to the vest had taken its toll, on both his psyche and his marriage. "Look," he admitted finally, "I will confide in you that I'm concerned."

"Shocker!"

"Our market share is eroding alarmingly, and even my stalwart performers like *Blue Justice* are not performing up to expectations."

"Well, isn't *Blue Justice* your fault? It used to be a gritty cop show, and now you let the two lead detectives move in with each other?"

Charles shrugged. "The two guys fell in love in real life. What could I do? Their deal was up. When an actor's deal is up you're pretty much obligated to do anything if you want to keep them in the fold."

"Gay cops."

"Well . . . there's nothing like it on television."

"Gee, I wonder why."

The thought of separate bedrooms was horrifying to Charles. "Sondy, I don't want to sleep without you . . . And moreover, when are we going to make love?"

"When do we make love *now*?"

"I'm usually ready Wednesday after the *Gersh* numbers come in."

Gersh was ABN's one megahit. It was far and away the number one show in the nation. Former stand-up Stevie Gersh and his cast of lovable losers trying to make it in Manhattan drew an audience of over thirty million weekly. Popular sitcoms like *Modern Family* and *The Big Bang Theory* had been left it its dust.

"We haven't had sex in a month," Sondra said.

Had it really been that long? A troubling thought occurred to Charles. "Well . . . why haven't you complained?"

"What's the point? It's sweeps."

Damage-control mode was becoming Charles Muncie's permanent state. "Tell you what. What if we make love right now?" He gestured to the phone. "Even with *those* numbers."

"Ooooh, that's so romantic."

"I'm serious."

Under the covers he began to play around, running his hand up her leg inside her nightie.

"What are you doing?"

"C'mon, let's celebrate us a little bit," Charles cooed.

"Charles, you woke me up from a deep sleep. And it's not *celebrating*, it's *fucking*. You're not addressing the affiliates."

"Sondy, like you said, it's been way too long," he said nibbling on her ear.

"Oh, all right," she sighed.

Charles would have preferred that she be more enthusiastic, but you play the cards you're dealt. He was now excited enough for the both of them. She peeled off her satin peach nightie. He wriggled quickly out of his boxers and took her in his arms.

"You know what your problem is?" she said. "And I'll tell you, it's going to kill you. You will not allow yourself even for a moment to accept the possibility of failure."

"Okay . . . so now I'm supposed to get an erection?"

"Seriously, Charles, you've done good work for ABN. You put on *Gersh* when everyone thought you were crazy."

If only she knew the truth about how *Gersh really* got on the air. But that was a secret he would take to his grave.

"Okay, you haven't been able to do that again, but how many *Gersh*'s are there? You can't stay on top forever."

"You're right. You can be on top tonight," he joked.

She smiled for the first time. Her husband was clearly making an effort. She gave him a "you're incorrigible" shake of the head and kissed him. They went back to being that ideal couple and began enjoying the best part of *being* a couple.

They made love efficiently more than passionately, but that was way good enough for Charles. And he figured if he got too excited too quickly he could just remember that his career, family's security, house, and entire self-worth all *did* depend on staying number one—forever.

But when that climax approached, he was able to stay swept up in the moment. "Oh yes!" he blurted out. "This is intimacy, a recognition of the heights that can be achieved when you and I commit to be us and celebrate our bounty of—"

The phone rang. Not his. The home phone.

"Fuck!"

"Oh, for crying out loud!" Sondra shouted, pushing Charles off her. "I thought you told them not to call this number."

Charles insisted that he had. This must be something else. He reached over and grabbed the phone.

"Hello?"

"Charles, you gotta come right over."

It was Stevie Gersh.

"What? Stevie? Now? It's five in the morning."

"I know. It's an emergency."

"Is this serious? Shouldn't you call 911?"

"I called *you*, damn it!"

"All right, all right." Charles could hear the urgency in Stevie's voice.

Stevie gave him directions to his beach house in the Malibu Colony.

"Fine. I'll be there in an hour."

"You can do better than that."

"I'm coming!"

He hung up the phone.

Charles despised Stevie Gersh with the white heat of a thousand suns. Stevie was an arrogant, self-centered prick who had no regard for anything or anyone else. Especially Charles. He took extra delight in humiliating the president of the network. Why? Because he *could*. Because at his core, Charles was a decent human being and Stevie saw that as a weakness to be exploited. Because Stevie always needed to have the upper hand. Again, because he *could*.

"What kind of emergency requires a network president at five o'clock in the morning?" Sondra asked.

"I don't know, but he told me to wear old clothes."

"Good night," she said and rolled over in bed.

"If we pick up where we left off it shouldn't take much time," Charles said hopefully.

Sondra fluffed up the pillow and closed her eyes. "Your things will be in the guest room by tonight."

CHAPTER 2

THE MALIBU COLONY was the superexclusive section of the already exclusive strip of beachfront property called Malibu (or just the "Bu"). Celebrities like Barbra Streisand, Jennifer Aniston, Stevie Gersh, Bruce Willis, and the old troubadour Bob Dylan resided in multimillion-dollar estates. All California beaches were public, but that didn't stop Colony resident David Geffen from walling off his section of sand and shore. Declaring that no one was above the law, not even billionaires, irate citizens came down on Geffen with the full force of justice, and twenty years later the walls were removed.

The only slight downside to living in the Malibu Colony was the occasional earthquake, wildfire, mudslide, and flooding due to battering surf during ferocious rainstorms. It was one of those impending storms that brought Charles Muncie to the "Bu" that early morning.

"You couldn't get anybody else to do this?"

Charles and Stevie were shoveling sand into burlap sacks at the water's edge. These were to be used to buttress Stevie's terrace from crashing waves.

In this day and age of only beautiful people on television, ABN's biggest star resembled a ferret wearing a Brillo Pad.

"Who else would answer his phone at this time of night?" Stevie asked while tying a bag.

"Well, who did Barbra Streisand call?"

"Who any fag hag would call—your two stars from *Blue Justice*."

Charles bristled. "Your malevolent insensitivity aside—"

"My what?"

"There is no other cop show on the air like it."

"You know what would be a better title? *Assume the Position.*"

Charles was not amused. Stevie dropped the topic.

"Okay, I'll be honest. I could've woken up my girlfriend, but she was sleeping so soundly. I was just being considerate."

A monster wave knocked Charles off his feet, ass over teakettle. Stevie reacted immediately. "This is not the time to take a dip. Dig! Dig!"

Charles emerged from the drink soaking wet and staggered to his feet. "Stevie, you've got like twelve sandbags. This is not going to help."

"Well," he said with a shrug, "if it doesn't, it doesn't. I'm probably going to sell it anyway."

Steam came out of Charles' ears.

"*You* interested in getting a place down here?"

Charles decided to just change the subject. "Tuesday night's show was a celebration of the best that television can be."

"*Celebration?* It's a sitcom, Charles. Not Jesus Christ being honored at the Kennedy Center."

"Yes, but I think you're really hitting your stride now," Charles said, suddenly realizing that he was shivering.

"Good. 'Cause that's the way I've always wanted to go out."

Charles stopped digging. "Go out? What do you mean?"

"Oh, that's the other reason I called you down here," Stevie said casually. "I'm done after this season."

"What?!" If the last wave had knocked Charles down, that statement was a tsunami. "You . . . you can't do that! You have the number one show in the country."

"Yeah, but my contract is up. I've done a hundred episodes, enough for syndication. I've done it. I've crossed the river Jordan. You've heard of *fuck you money*? I have *fuck God money*."

"But what about your artistic need to create? To be a major driving force in popular culture?"

"Ehhh, you get tired of that. Look, I'll move on to other things.

I don't know *what*, but I just know I need a rest from being funny."

It was all Charles could do to not vomit into his sandbag. "Stevie, I understand that the work is arduous. Who was it who said, 'Dying is hard; comedy is harder'?"

"Christ, I believe."

"The point is you have every right to feel fatigued, to want a well-deserved respite—"

"Or Carrot Top."

"Huh? What? Would you please listen, Stevie? This is an important matter. What I'm endeavoring to say is that yes, there is great effort involved, but the rewards are so much greater. And this is the best time of your life. You will look back and forget the struggles. You will just remember what a golden period it was—a period that can never be recaptured."

"What about Tim Allen?" Stevie wondered.

"*Last Man Standing* wasn't nearly as successful as *Home Improvement*," answered Charles.

"No. I mean who said the thing about dying and comedy."

"Goddammit, Stevie! Do you mind? It's not enough I'm standing here sopping wet? I have to be your straight man, too?"

Stevie liked to push people to see how far he could go. But he knew when to back off. Usually it was when the person said, "Back off!"

"Listen, dude. I just see things from a different perspective. Willie Mays."

"Willie Mays never said anything about comedy. I don't understand," Charles said.

"No. Now *I'm* making a point. Willie Mays was the greatest ballplayer of his age."

"Arguable but okay."

"But did you ever see him at the end of his career? Playing for the Mets. He was a fucking whale. Way overweight. Stumbling around in the outfield, dropping fly balls he would have caught in his hip pocket a few years before. It's like the great Willie Mays became Cedric the Entertainer. And then there's the immortal Joe Louis—

the world's greatest prizefighter—and what ultimately happened to him at the end? He was a fucking greeter in Las Vegas. And by then he'd been hit in the head so many times he probably didn't remember his own name much less anyone he met. Charles, my man, there's nothing more pathetic than a guy who doesn't know when to leave. Keep digging."

Now it dawned on Charles. A small smile crossed his frozen lips. "Okay, let's cut to it because I don't want this going any further than here. You tell me, right now, what do you want? Whatever it is makes no difference. I know I'm not putting myself in a good bargaining position, but you've got it. I'll do anything."

Stevie laughed. "Charles, I have it all. I don't need money, future commitments, a statue in front of ABN. There is nothing you can do for me that will change this."

"Nothing?"

"You could let me sleep with your wife; it wouldn't make me change my mind."

Charles was practically apoplectic. "Stevie, you . . . you can't quit. There's more to this than just you."

Stevie shook his head. "Charles, you don't get it. To me, there's *just* me."

CHAPTER 3

CHARLES STAGGERED BACK HOME at about noon—distraught, sticky, sandy, and smelling like a Rubio's fish taco that had been left in a hot car for a week. Unfortunately, there was no time to shower because Kelly Rose's soccer game began promptly at twelve thirty. This was a weekly ritual. Charles and Sondra would go to Brentwood Park to watch their daughter compete in a USYS organized soccer game.

The kids were warming up and the parents were staking out their spots on the sidelines. All the moms and dads were dressed in the latest sports apparel. They all had iPads (God forbid they were bored for one second) and portable lawn chairs so that no one had to actually sit on the grass. The mommies were all in their thirties. The daddies were all in their thirties or sixties.

Charles stood, trying to situate himself where there was the maximum breeze.

A fellow parent, Jason, crossed by. "Hey, Charles, *Gersh* was a fuckin' riot this week," he said.

"Thank you," Charles mustered.

"I mean, seriously, that guy is an absolute genius."

Charles held up his hand. "I appreciate your interest and patronage, but please, this is my Saturday. I like to think of soccer as my sanctuary from work and I cherish these private moments very, very much."

"Jeez, sorry, I was paying you a compliment. The rest of your shows are shit. Have a nice *sanctuary*."

Jason walked away, shaking his head.

"Oh hell!" Charles said, looking across the field. "Is that that Marc Jantzen? *He's* living in this neighborhood now?"

Marc Jantzen was the newly appointed president of Fox. Thanks to the phone-hacking scandal that swept out half the executives above him, Jantzen was able to rocket up the corporate ladder. Unlike Charles, he had an easy charm—one that didn't require mantras to keep him centered. And it didn't hurt that at thirty-four he looked like Justin Timberlake at twenty-seven.

Jantzen had vowed that he would turn Fox around in one year, and his first target was ABN because it was clearly the most vulnerable of the major networks. Sharks smell blood in the water and gay cops were blood.

Here he was on this overcast Saturday, complete with his obligatory gorgeous wife and von Trapp children.

So much for Charles' *sanctuary.*

"You're being silly," Sondra said. "It's no big deal. Be the bigger man and walk over and say hello."

But just as she said this, Marc crossed the field, beating Charles to the punch.

They exchanged pleasantries. God, Marc had white teeth close up.

"Jesus," Marc said, scrunching his nose, "where have you been? Recruiting writers from a homeless shelter?"

"I was helping Stevie Gersh fill sandbags," Charles said proudly.

"Why?"

"He lives in Malibu and there's an impending storm."

"No. Why you?"

"It's the kind of personal service I give to all of my network family."

Marc stuffed his hands in his designer jean pockets. "Gee, Charles, now you make me feel bad. Mindy Kaling's toilet overflowed and I didn't run out of a staff meeting with a plunger."

Charles forced a laugh, much as he would do in response to some oaf affiliate station owner from West Virginia who just told a joke about a bear raping a hunter.

"Hey, I just bought a house up on Bristol Circle," Marc continued.

"Oh. That's above me."

"Yeah, I can probably look right down into your backyard."

Inside, Charles bristled. "I doubt that," he said. "I have a grove of indigenous oaks surrounding my property."

"Oh yes, the one on the corner. Hope you don't hot tub in the nude, 'cause from my bedroom I can look right down into your pool area."

"Well . . . we don't . . . anymore." Charles sighed.

Marc draped his arm around Charles. He was four inches taller than him. "Isn't this job a hoot?" he asked.

Always the diplomat, Charles responded with, "Yes, well, I too celebrate the opportunity to be a broadcaster."

"Huh? I said I'm having *fun.*"

"I have fun," Charles protested. "I might even submit that I have more fun than you."

Marc chuckled. "What you *have*, pal, is *Gersh.*"

"And you don't. So that constitutes fun."

That was lame, he realized immediately.

"Right. I guess. Well, have a good game. Please shower before we move in next week. The wind sometimes blows north." Marc patted him on the back and strolled away.

There were always people gunning for you. That was part of the job. Charles understood that. But there was something different about Marc Jantzen. More disconcerting. More ominous. More formidable. Charles made a mental note to keep a closer eye on Marc and ask his development VPs whether "People You Hate" might be the germ of a great new reality show.

****

Later that night, banished to the guest room, Charles stared up at the ceiling from his Thompson twin while Sondra slept soundly in the master bedroom in their big California king. He tried to contemplate life after *Gersh*, and the prospect was scary. He got out of bed and padded down the hallway to his home office to review his pilot scripts. The lifeblood of any television network is its development department. New hits must replace old hits, so millions of dollars are spent each year on commissioning scripts for potential new series and filming pilots for the scripts that show the most promise. It's an inexact science, as is evidenced by the ninety-five percent failure rate for new shows.

And determining good projects from bad was not Charles Muncie's strong suit. In fact, it was his glaring weakness. He was a good politician, projected that aura of calm (although at the expense of his internal organs), and maintained good relationships within the creative community.

But picking shows? He was still getting grief for the Ann Coulter family comedy.

The key feature of Charles' home office was his bank of television monitors—six of them—which took up an entire wall and were enclosed in a handsome oak cabinet. One master remote controlled them all, along with six DVRs, two Blu-rays, and an ancient VCR. Every week Charles called the engineering department to ask them to remind him how to record shows again. A glass-topped desk sat across the room, filled with stacks of scripts, and in the corner, propped up on an easel, was a large magnetic display board with a grid for days and time slots. Multicolored magnetic strips representing every show on the five networks' schedules adorned the whiteboard.

All the TVs were on when Charles entered the room. He grabbed the remote to turn them all off. This took five minutes, since he inadvertently changed channels six times, started two recordings, and ejected a movie from one of the Blu-rays.

He reread the pilot scripts all night, hoping that one of them would be his savior. Snoop Dogg as an international lawyer? Former mob boss now is a party clown? None of them sounded any good. Although how would he know? The worst pilot he ever read was for a show called *Gersh*. Just a steaming pile of mean, distasteful jokes, unlikable characters, and a star who looked too Jewish for Jews, much less Middle America. That it even got on the air at all was a fluke. Staring at the magnetic board, Charles recalled the circumstances.

It was four years ago, when Charles was a rookie president. He was in his New York office, high above Manhattan, finalizing his fall schedule. After a week of consultation with his staff, reviewing all the research data, and fending off lobbying agents and studios, he had locked it in.

It was one a.m. He would proudly announce it to the world tomorrow and second-guess himself for the next four months.

Lana Herring, his trusty assistant, had poked her head in. She never went home until he did. Lana was Charles' age, dark auburn hair pulled back into a ponytail—she was somewhere between *attractive* and *character actress*.

Lana believed in Charles and was very loyal to him. She sensed a conscience underneath the corporate exterior. That was a rare commodity for a television executive any higher than assistant commissary manager. She had a little crush on Charles but never acted upon it. Charles Muncie was the most happily married man she knew. Lana would have to be content with her boyfriend, who was a *non-pro*. That was the Hollywood trade papers' expression for someone not in the entertainment business. In other words, someone worthless. Mahatma Gandhi was a non-pro.

Lana entered the office with trepidation. Charles stood before the display board, just staring at it. Not even blinking. His mind was a blur. Was this the best schedule? Other than the Ann Coulter family comedy, were there any other surefire new hits? When would he hear if Kelly Rose got into that preschool they wanted? How the hell could *America's Funniest Home Videos* still be on the air? Hey, the skyline from his office looked like the opening titles from the old *Amos 'n' Andy* show. In pressure situations Charles' head was often a jumble of indecision, ambition, and God knew what.

"Charles?" Lana said tentatively. But it was enough to startle him.

"Huh? What? Oh." He quickly shifted into Mr. Confidence mode.

"I have some bad news. Your mother had a heart attack."

"Mother? Oh my God!" Charles was visibly shaken. "Get me on a plane to Atlanta. Call my wife. Lana, this is the third one. I think this might be it. I want to be by her side, and I don't want to be disturbed. For anything."

"Of course."

"Breckman can announce the schedule tomorrow."

"I'll call him."

"All too often work commandeers our private lives and distorts our priorities. Even though I'm indispensible, there's nothing that you or my team can't handle."

"Right."

"I'm even leaving my cell phone. This is now 'Mom time' for the duration."

"I'll handle everything. I'm so sorry."

"Thank you. Bless her heart for holding on until I figured out what to do with Thursdays."

Charles shoved his iPhone into a desk drawer, then dashed out of the office. Lana followed, passing Ernesto, the maintenance man, coming in to clean Charles' office. Ernesto began to vacuum and accidentally bumped the magnetic board. A couple of strips were jarred loose and floated to the ground. The last thing Ernesto needed was to be written up, so he did the best he could to put the strips back in their original spots. Maybe no one would notice. One of the strips he retrieved from the ground said *Gersh*. Ernesto Escardon Jr. from Washington Heights put *Gersh* at nine o'clock on Tuesdays nights.

Where it has remained for one hundred classic episodes.

Charles swept aside the scripts and slumped back in his chair. Who was he kidding? There was no in-house solution. He had to keep *Gersh*. It was as simple and complicated as that.

CHAPTER 4

TWO YEARS AGO, Global United Industries—makers of . . . just about everything—added ABN to their ledger. Chairman of the communications division Leonard Armantrout (who oversaw ABN, Globecast cable, Vid-demand.com, Globe Cinemas, and the Dick Clark American Bandstand Diners in the Phoenix and Newark airports) was not a fan of Charles Muncie. It was Charles' misfortune to bear a close resemblance to his idiot son-in-law who wrote self-published novels.

Every month Charles was summoned to New York to provide a status report and get a whipping.

There was a Global United Industries corporate jet. It just always seemed to be "busy" whenever Charles needed it. Obama never had to fly to New York and back commercial because Michelle was using Air Force One to take the kids to camp. Charles did fly first class at least, but that was stipulated in his contract. Otherwise, he figured, Global United would cheerfully have him fly coach, with stops in Denver and Minneapolis. Still, the indignity. And worse, nothing but Fox shows as part of their in-flight so-called entertainment.

This recent quick trip to New York had been brutal. Charles sipped a glass of airline-vintage wine and checked his watch. Four more hours until LAX.

He had spent the better part of two days being told by Leonard Armantrout and the board of directors things he already knew. When Global purchased ABN they were number one in the eighteen-to-thirty-four demographic by a full four percent. Now less than one percent. Charles tried to point out some positives but was forever interrupted by Armantrout, who was quite blunt. "Charles, you made quite a career for yourself off of the success of *Gersh*. I suggest you find a way to make the same magic happen again. You've got one year to turn this around and put us back where we rightfully belong. One year."

"Consider it done. One year is very doable," Charles said. "And I appreciate your candor."

He hated that he was given an ultimatum, but at least Armantrout had the decency to be straight with him and not just tell him the board was behind him and then start interviewing other candidates as soon as he hit the elevator. So he had a year. Actually six months. Armantrout wasn't *that* honest.

Of course, what difference did it make? The minute Stevie Gersh announced he was quitting, eight interns would be packing Charles' things. He wouldn't be surprised to walk into his LA office tomorrow and find two of his vice presidents there with tape measures. But Charles was proud of himself. He managed to put up a good front. He was "in charge," Kennedy during the Cuban missile crisis (before learning that Kennedy was on meth at the time).

"Was there anything else, Leonard?" he asked.

"Yes, there is. You know the actress Katherine Heigl? Some of the fellas here would like to meet her."

Charles' attention was quickly jolted back to the present when the plane was rocked by unexpected clear-air turbulence. At least it was white wine and not red that he spilled on his pants. For Charles Muncie lately, that was a *lucky* day. The pilot came on the PA and in that now-FAA-standard Chuck Yeager drawl suggested everyone strap on their seat belts or they were going to be hitting "the friendly roof."

The turbulence continued . . . and never let up. Passengers were screaming, filling airsick bags, and dropping into the fetal position. The passengers in the exit rows who had so cavalierly agreed to assist airline personnel in case of an emergency in exchange for their added legroom now had serious misgivings. The flight attendants did a head count and noticed two people were not in their seats. Where were they? That mystery was solved when a horrible banging began from one of the restrooms as if two cats had been trapped in a clothes dryer. Welcome to the worst mile high club ever.

The turbulence continued for four straight hours. Charles and the rest of the jostled passengers staggered off the plane at Los Angeles International at ten a.m. looking like the cast of *The Walking Dead* only not as frisky. Two minutes later, Charles was in the men's room on his knees throwing up for probably the tenth time. His iPhone rang. Charles wanted to ignore it but saw who was calling. Swell! He slid his finger across the screen. "Hello, Stevie. Could you just give me a moment?" He heaved one last time, then: "Thank you. Listen, Stevie, to be honest, I'm in a meeting."

Like that meant anything to Stevie Gersh. "Yeah, great. Listen, I've got something to tell you, but I don't want to do it over the phone. I need you to come over here."

"Can it wait?" Charles asked, knowing the answer.

"No! What part of 'get over here now' didn't you understand?"

"You never said 'get over here *now*.'"

"Jesus Christ, Charles! The very fact that I called—it's *implied*! Who calls and says come on over and expects that it means later or at your convenience?"

Every other person on the planet was what Charles wanted to answer, but instead he just mumbled, "Okay. Fine."

All Charles wanted to do was to crawl into his bed and beg for death, but he dutifully agreed to drive right out to Malibu.

"Malibu? I'm not in Malibu."

No, he was not. An hour later, the president of ABN was back in the air on a flight to Boston, Massachusetts—and encountering the same rockin' and rollin' he'd faced flying west. The cabin bounced like a cocktail shaker. And since Charles had booked the flight so late, the only seats available were in coach. If you think it's bumpy in row two, row forty-six is like riding a mechanical bull. And the on-board entertainment was no distraction. When they weren't showing Fox shows, they screened *Bridesmaids*.

Charles crawled to the waiting limousine at Logan International Airport at seven p.m. The driver was a native Bostonian who drove like one. Whoa, Nellie! It was Mr. Toad's Wild Ride! Who drag races through Government Square in a stretch limo? They lurched to a sudden stop in front of the Bull & Finch Pub—better known as Cheers.

The driver opened the back door and Charles almost tumbled out onto the street. With legs of jelly he gingerly walked down that familiar street-level flight of stairs. Inside, Stevie was at a small table waiting for him.

The actual Cheers bar is very similar to the one seen on television but much smaller and cozier, and the bar itself is pushed against the back wall, not in the center of the room. Were it in the center Charles would have slammed into it and probably knocked himself out as he zigzagged across to Stevie. But the décor is the same as what you see on the show: brick walls, stained glass windows, wooden tables, framed photos. The main theme here is selling *Cheers* products, and in the adjacent gift shop you can buy *Cheers* mugs, shirts, photos, DVDs—probably even Sam Malone condoms.

Charles waded through the tourists and joined Stevie at a corner table under a Tiffany lamp.

"Jesus!" Stevie said with a laugh. "You look like Dr. Emmett Brown in *Back to the Future*."

"It was a very rugged flight."

"I should say. So you hungry?"

"Hungry? Are you kidding? Look at me. I've just relived every meal I've had for the last four days."

"Well, they have great sliders, so I just had to ask."

Charles groaned. What was more nauseating, he wondered—the thought of eating greasy little cheeseburgers or just listening to Stevie Gersh?

"Cheer up, Chuckles. I'm about to make your trip all worth it." Stevie paused for effect.

Charles was in no mood for suspense. "What?" he snapped.

"I've decided to do the show a couple more years."

Charles eyes widened like saucers. It was like the ceiling opened, a beam of golden light shot down from the heavens, and a celestial chorus of angels sang "Ava Maria" or "Love Shack."

Charles was saved! He was so ecstatic his face went from green to pink. The weight of the world had been lifted from his shoulders.

"Thank you, Stevie. I can't begin to express the exultation I'm feeling at this moment. And not just for me. For the thirty million people whose lives will be enriched for . . . are we talking one year or two?"

"That's yet to be determined."

"Fine. We'll work that out. Let's just celebrate this moment."

"So, Charles, before you said that if I'd re-sign you would do anything. Did you mean that?"

"Yes. Unequivocally."

"I'll let the lawyers work out the money."

"I thought you said you weren't interested in money."

"I'm not, but since we're going ahead with this, hey, you might as well pay me more than anyone has ever gotten for any show ever."

"Right," Charles said cautiously.

"But that's not what will close the deal. What I really need is for you to do something for me personally," Stevie said quietly.

"Of course," said Charles, relieved. Goody. If it was personal, it wouldn't be something he'd have to run by the board.

The non-pro, who looked more like Norm than like Diane or Carla, approached to take Charles' order and remind them both that *Cheers* logo iPhone cases were on sale for only seventeen fifty, today only. Normally they were twenty-five dollars. Charles just ordered some water. Did he want it in a cool *Cheers* KOR water bottle for only thirty-two dollars? No. Just the water in a generic noncollectable glass. The non-pro moved on.

Stevie glanced around the room for a moment, then leaned in to Charles. "This is about Lucy."

Lucy Adamson was Stevie's girlfriend. Late twenties, very sweet, Jennifer Love Hewitt with a little meat on her bones. Charles really liked Lucy. She seemed to have a very calming effect on Stevie. "I've got to tell you, " Charles said, "I see the look in your eyes when you're with her and it's not your usual 'nothing breaks through this comic façade.'"

Stevie took a swig of his imported ale. "Well, for once, Charles, you're right. It's been about a year now, the last three months even monogamous. For the first time in my life I'm in love. Real love." As if to really make the point: "The kind where you have moments of putting the happiness of the other person ahead of yours."

"Stevie, this is so—"

"Yeah, yeah, you *celebrate* me."

The non-pro returned with Charles' order. "Here ya go, mister," she said in a thick Boston accent. "Just like the water they drank on the show." She moved off to annoy someone else. Stevie launched back into the story.

"So last week I brought her back east. I have my place on the Cape. It's bigger than James Taylor's. So picture this, Charles—I take her out on my fifty-foot sailboat. I bought it from Michael J. Fox. Can you just see him steering a sailboat?"

Stevie mimicked this, which only made the joke more distasteful and horrifying.

"Anyway, I took her to this private cove. And I had it all set up. A table for two on the sand. Candlelight. A bottle of champagne. A staff standing by to serve us a sumptuous dinner. Even had a violinist. Hey, can you imagine Michael J. Fox trying to play a violin?"

"Stevie! Please, just go on with your . . . rapturous story," implored Charles.

"Right. We arrive. It's sunset. The sky is incredible. Shades of purple and gold—the most amazing sunset you've ever seen. Like something out of . . . *The Bachelor.* So I dock the boat . . . well, the staff docked the boat. But I took her hand, led her to the table, and I gotta tell you, she was blown away. What chick wouldn't be? I poured the champagne; it was perfect. And then do you know what I did?"

Probably sodomized her in front of the staff was what Charles thought. But instead he just said, "No."

"I got down on one knee. And proposed."

"Really? You proposed marriage to Lucy Adamson?" Charles was shocked and delighted.

"That's right. I showed her the ring. And it was huge, lemme tell ya. A rock the size of a water tumbler."

"That's very . . . sentimental."

"I gave her my heart . . ."

"Stevie, I am so happy for you."

"And the bitch turned me down!"

"What?"

"She said no. She was very flattered and all—like that makes it okay—but she saw her life a certain way and I didn't fit that."

Charles had two immediate thoughts. He needed to be very delicate in how he handled this matter. And good for Lucy for not wanting to marry this shitheel.

"Well, you live a formidable one, Stevie, and you have quite a reputation."

"No, it's not that. I think she's in love with someone else."

"How do you know that?"

"Come on. What else could it *be*, for godsakes?"

"A lot of things."

Stevie leaned in, almost nose to nose. "She. Doesn't. Want. Me. Charles!"

Got it. Message received. Stevie dramatically swept Charles' water glass off the table, where it shattered on the ground. For a split second Charles felt a pang of empathy for him. But then he remembered the callous Michael J. Fox jokes and thought, *Serves you right, you egomaniacal prick.* What he said, though, was, "Stevie, I'm so profoundly sorry. What can I—what can *we* at ABN—do to ease your pain?"

"Kill her."

Charles nodded. "I know how you must feel," he said softly, patting his hand, "but really, we're here for you."

Stevie locked eyes with Charles. "No, I mean it. I want her off the fucking earth! That's why I came to you. I want you to handle it.

Whatever you have to do, do it, and I'll sign up for another two years. Aw hell, make it *three*. You're taking a life."

Charles stared at him in utter disbelief. Stevie repeated that that was the condition and wondered if Charles wanted to see a movie that night.

After a long moment, Charles was finally able to compose words and respond. "Y'know, Stevie, it's one thing for you to humiliate me in public . . ."

Just last month at the *Gersh* one-hundredth-episode party, Stevie sat Charles in a large sheet cake as flashbulbs popped and video cameras rolled. Recently the YouTube video of that *uproarious* incident reached one million views.

". . . and to make ass-fun of me on all the late-night shows. It's another to drag me three thousand miles to play a practical joke. Goddammit, I'm a network president! I have better things to do than this. Now, I'm here to offer you a blank check. I'm here to offer you stock options in the parent company. I mean, every time some dickhead pops open a soft drink you make a nickel. A home in Aspen. Tee times at Augusta National . . . well, at least this year while we still have the Masters. Just tell me what the fuck you want from me!"

"I want you to kill Lucy Adamson."

"Stop it!" Charles was furious now.

"You have three weeks. My writers and I need the time to come up with a really good final show."

Charles grabbed Stevie by the shoulders. "What's going on here? It's like I don't know you."

"I've never proposed and been turned down before," Stevie said, almost as an afterthought.

Charles released him. He leaned back in his chair. "Do you really think for one minute that I would ever do something like that?"

"Guess it depends on how much you need me, " the star of *Gersh* said with a shrug.

It finally sank in. Holy Mother of God! This man was *serious*. A chill ran up Charles' spine. What else was there to say except "You are one disturbed individual."

"Maybe," Stevie said, getting up from the table, "but thirty million people a week love me."

Charles couldn't move. He was stunned. Shell-shocked. Stevie started out but turned back for one parting shot. "The *Cheers* bar. Where would NBC have been without *Cheers*? Have a nice flight home."

CHAPTER 5

EVERYONE IN HOLLYWOOD goes to a shrink. So all the craziness you see in la-la land—that's *with* therapy. Charles had been seeing Dr. David Gold. Dr. Gold was very popular within the industry because he offered sound advice and his office was a separate little cottage in his backyard in Beverly Hills, accessible from an alley. Celebrities and high-profile executives could slip in and out unnoticed. Even some patients who disagreed with everything he advised still went to Dr. Gold because of his location.

Charles sat across from his therapist. Typical Hollywood shrink, he was a man in his fifties wearing blue jeans.

"You're not going to kill anybody," Dr. Gold said.

"I didn't say I was," Charles answered.

Show business patients asked permission for all sorts of reprehensible behavior. The rule of thumb was if you made a movie that grossed over two hundred million you believed you were entitled to one felony.

"I was just making the point that my counterparts probably would. Without hesitation. And I find that appalling, both on moral levels and because I hate to give others an advantage."

"Then let me ask you—why on earth would you even want to be in this business?"

"I love television," Charles said, launching into a reverie. "I always have. I spent hours alone in my room watching it. I came from a dysfunctional home. An unhappy father and a passive-aggressive mother. You know—*America*.

"Is it too much of a cliché to say I used television as an escape from harsh reality?" Charles wondered.

"Yes, but in your case it applies."

Charles nodded, satisfied. He also wondered why every psychiatrist in Los Angeles decorated his office with a Southwest theme. Was there a bulk-rate sale on Navajo rugs? But that he didn't wonder aloud.

"I couldn't get enough television, " Charles continued. "School, of course, provided the important vitamins and minerals for my intellect. My friends provided"—he needed a moment to find the right word—"*fiber*. But it was television. All those inspirational programs. *ALF. Dynasty. The Scarecrow and Mrs. King.* Television provided the *taste* that made it all go down."

Dr. Gold shifted in his oversized leather chair. "You're kind of all over the place metaphorically, but I catch your drift."

Early on Charles knew that television was his calling, that somehow he had to get into the industry.

"My dilemma was that early on I discovered that I couldn't write or act. But just because I couldn't make the shows didn't mean I couldn't at least put them in order.

"I've been very fortunate. I've risen to the absolute zenith of my profession. And I take my responsibility seriously. I have the rare precious opportunity to provide amelioration and enlightenment to millions of viewers. Oh, if there was only a way to continue my sacred commitment to humanity without murdering someone."

It was time for a different tack. "How are things between you and Sondra?" Dr. Gold asked.

Charles squirmed and crossed his legs. "I'm sleeping in the guest room because I scream four mornings a week. Things between us are slipping away. I'm never home. And when I am, Sondra says I'm always distracted. That's not true. How long have you had that Navajo carpet?"

"How long has it been since you've had sex?"

"*Completed* sex?"

"Yes."

"Two months."

"Does that bother you?"

"Well, of course. It's communion with my wife. It's at the very least a release from the thousand and one tensions that occupy me at every moment."

"Well, can't you gently tell her that?"

"The truth is, I have broached the subject, but to no avail. It's as if she's lost some feeling for me. For her, it's just sex for the sake of sex. Which would still be okay if we actually *had* sex."

"Well, you clearly need physical and emotional reinforcement," Dr. Gold offered. "Have you ever thought of an affair?"

Charles recoiled a bit. "You're telling me to do that? That's okay for psychiatrists to do?"

"I'm telling you that I'm beginning to worry about you. And before you do something stupid like even entertaining this killing notion for one second, I think it would be a much more healthy situation for you to find a woman who is attracted to you and have an affair. I present that only as an alternative."

"I could never do that," Charles stated piously. "That just isn't me."

"Fine."

"And even if it were—actresses would want favors, you don't shit where you eat, and hookers would tell Charlie Sheen."

Obviously there were other options, but Charles' time was up.

CHAPTER 6

A GOOD COMPROMISE was a massage.

Charles climbed aboard the portable massage table, head through the face cradle, wearing only a towel. Soft New Age music wafted through the sound system in Charles' office. He wondered if it was John Tesh. He had hired Tesh just two years before to host a pilot, *Battle of the Network Reality Judges*, that didn't go. But this was not a time to be thinking of television. Or murdering anyone. This was a time to celebrate peace and relaxation. Charles instructed Lana to hold his calls for an hour as Anji DeVelera—highly recommended by his sports division—gave him a good-deep tissue massage.

Twenty-nine-year-old Anji (pronounced *On-gee*) was every middle-aged man's dream. Classic California beauty—golden blond, golden tan, killer body, neon smile, and a warm, bubbly personality that played right into the fantasy that she actually liked you. Or at least knew you were in the room.

Charles moaned silently as she dug her palms into his upper back.

"Boy, you're really tight," she said.

"Who couldn't use a good massage?" he answered.

"No. Really. *Really* tight. As in how do you move?"

"There's very little difference between deciding whether to attack Libya and letting Adele star in a comedy. Well . . . actually there *is*, but you get the point. There's a tremendous amount of pressure being a president."

Anji's eyes lit up. "You're *the president*?"

The giant corner office didn't give it away? This was not a Mensa member. Still, the excitement in her voice gave him a little charge. As modestly as he could, he confirmed that indeed he was the president (and would remain so as long as an innocent young lady was found with a bullet in her head).

Anji was almost breathless.

"All my favorite shows are on ABN. And you're, like, the dude who comes up with them?" she gushed.

"Well, yes, I'm the . . . dude." He lied modestly. She was very impressed.

"I really want to get into television in some way," Anji said.

Jackpot! Most people in this town who were non-pros wanted desperately to be pros.

"Hopefully, in front of the camera. But I don't know how to go about that."

If ever there was an invitation, that was it. And Charles was very tempted. Anji wore tight shorts and a halter top that barely restrained her full natural breasts. He considered the prospect very seriously, then answered, "Well, work hard and, uh, believe in yourself. Get some good eight-by-tens taken, get an agent, then start cultivating the fields. Same old story." Charles opted for the high road and was very pleased with himself . . . and was also kicking himself for being such a schmuck.

"I already have eight-by-tens," Anji chirped. "I had them taken in Hawaii. Bikini shots mostly. I was there competing in the Ms. Fitness America Contest. Just a bunch of us fair-haired hard bodies trying to get noticed."

He moaned again, louder this time. "Well . . . it also helps to have some support. A family, boyfriend . . . that sort of thing." Clearly Mr. High Road was fishing.

"My family is back in Chicago, and right now there's no man. I'm just . . . out there."

All the while she'd been sensuously running her strong hands up and down his now-quivering body. And, he realized, he hadn't thought about homicide in at least two minutes.

Buzzzzz! The mood was shattered by Lana coming in on the intercom. "Charles? I know you said no calls, but Mr. Armantrout is on line two from New York."

"Shit! Okay. Put him through." Talk about a mood kill. What fresh hell was *this*? he wondered.

Charles reached over and activated the speakerphone. The muffled foghorn of Leonard Armantrout filled the room. "Charles. I just heard a distressing rumor. Do you know anything about Stevie Gersh wanting out after this season?"

Now, where the fuck had he heard that? It was amazing. No one could keep a secret in this industry. Three thousand miles away and a guy who primarily oversees aluminum production found out about it.

Charles once again had to lock into his pseudo Zen-like calm damage-control mode. "What? No. Where did you hear that?"

"I've just been hearing it."

Asshole. Wouldn't even say.

"That's news to me."

"You're sure?"

"Leonard, rumors fly all the time. All I know is what I hear from the man himself. And he told me at the one-hundredth party . . ."

"The one where he threw you into the cake?"

Anji giggled.

"What was that?"

Anji clasped her mouth. Charles signaled that it was all right. "A laugh track. Sorry. I'm screening a show."

"Thank you," Anji mouthed. What a sweet guy Charles was. Most executives would have been furious.

"But yes, the cake," Charles said. "Stevie and I are close enough buds that he can do that. What do the kids call it? A bromance? Anyway, he told me that as long as I'm here, he's ready to do a hundred more."

"Good," snarled the CEO. "Because without *Gersh* we will be in free fall, and if we are, you'll be the one hitting the ground first."

Yes, he really had to remind Charles of the precarious position he was in because otherwise he would have forgotten. Like in *24* when Jack Bauer would constantly badger Chloe over the phone that he needed those schematics now or the bomb was going to explode and wipe out half the city. It didn't sink in the first five times. If Jack hadn't said anything she might've taken her break.

"Will it rain tomorrow?" Charles answered breezily. "I worry about that more."

"Good enough," Armantrout said, clearly not assuaged. "Oh . . . and still waiting on Katherine Heigl."

Charles reached over and hung up the phone, thinking to himself how sad it was that these old guys were chasing after young hotties.

"I'm so sorry," Anji said. "I didn't mean to get you in trouble. It just slipped out."

"No worries at all. In this town, as long as I beat CBS I could run a Chinese slave trade operation out of my office."

Anji giggled and said, "You are like the sweetest guy ever!"

"I don't know if that's technically true, but thank you." Charles was finding the high road had a lot of steep curves.

"Oh, while you were on the phone, I dug up a handout on good nutrition—which is vital to supergood health—and my eight-by-tens." She showed them to him. "There I am. Anji DeVelera."

And they were spectacular. If for no other reason than to save a life (for Armantrout had really backed him into a corner), Charles said, "Anji, are you free tomorrow?"

CHAPTER 7

YOU COULDN'T BE TOO CAREFUL. Not in Hollywood. Not with *TMZ* bottom-feeders lurking in every garbage disposal and alley. Not when you leafed through *Us* magazine at your doctor's office and there were exclusive photos of Kiernan Shipka buying tampons. *ET is there* whether they were invited or not. Gossipmonger *Perez* Hilton had become more well-known than *Paris* Hilton.

And that was just the trivial stuff. Nothing sold like scandal, and there was no shortage of sordid affairs and deviant behavior in the Wet Dream Factory. Back in the thirties and forties, major movie studios had people on salary whose sole profession was to clean up and hide the mess. Oscar-winning leading men could sleep with starlets, harlots, piglets, and choirboys and no one would know despite all the fan magazines and gossip columnists of the day. People were roughed up, careers ruined, lives threatened—it was a golden time. Stevie could kill Lucy himself and get away with it back then.

But today every phone was a video camera, any idiot could have a blog, and since no deterrent was going to stop entitled human beings from having sex, an entire multimillion-dollar industry had arisen out of soiled bedsheets.

So Charles Muncie, president of ABN, had to take extra precautions. There was no just slipping into the Four Seasons or Century Plaza Hotel. He needed a more out-of-the-way location for his little tryst.

After extensive late-night online research (and deleting his search history), the Courtyard by Marriott in San Bernardino was selected.

Clean, discreet, and free Wi-Fi.

His fern gray Jaguar roared into the parking lot. The hotel looked liked every other Courtyard by Marriott. Charles sat in the car and waited. Eleven twenty-five a.m. Several anxious moments later a red Toyota Camry puttered in. Charles smiled. He wasn't certain she'd come. And since the hotel was about a mile off the freeway and required *both* right- and left-hand turns, he wasn't sure she'd find it. But she did. Anji was here! She climbed out of her import wearing red short shorts and a yellow sports bra. Charles, in his navy suit, got out of the Jag and met her.

They hugged; he thanked her for coming and for being so understanding. At $4.69 a gallon, she'd used a half a tank to get here. Charles offered to cover her travel expenses.

Clearly, he was a little nervous. He had been married for nine years and had never done anything like this. For the first seven years, he never even *considered* it.

Anji was willing to let him off the hook. "We don't have to, you know," she said, her breasts practically falling out of the bra.

"No, no," replied Charles stoically. "We're here."

Anji perked up. "Awesome. So let's go get sweaty! Wooooh!"

Charles gently grabbed her elbow to delay her. "Tell you what. Why don't you stay in the car? I'll get the room. Then I'll go up and call you with the room number. Here, take my cell phone."

Anji blew right past him. "Oh, come on. No one's going to see you."

He took a deep breath, then followed her inside to the reception desk. The lobby was empty. A good sign. Who stayed at the Courtyard by Marriott in San Bernardino anyway? What was there to do or see? The two big attractions in the town were the first McDonald's location and an indoor karting raceway.

The non-pro at the reception desk was a somewhat officious stork in his fifties. He welcomed them to the Courtyard, "here in the very heart of the great Inland Empire," and Charles told him they had a reservation.

"It's under the name Phelps. Jim Phelps."

The clerk chuckled. "Jim Phelps? You know you have the same name as that guy on *Mission Impossible*?"

Charles silently cursed himself for choosing that name. He should've used the dad on *ALF*. But he deftly explained to the non-pro that he'd taken a lot of ribbing.

"Well, Mr. Phelps, your mission, should you decide to accept it, is to fill out this form and—"

"Will you please stop that?"

"Sorry. Is that your colleague Cinnamon? Last time. I promise. Now, if I could just have your credit card."

"I'll pay in cash." Charles couldn't afford to leave a paper trail.

"Still, Mr. Phelps. That's hotel policy. Once you settle the bill and pay in full, the credit card slip will be ripped up."

Still, Charles worried that the information might remain somewhere in the system.

"What if I paid you the cash up front?"

"Your name isn't really Phelps, is it?"

"Yes, it is!" he snapped. "I'm Jim Phelps. Please give me a minute."

Charles took Anji aside and spoke to her in a hushed tone.

"Could you pay with your credit card and then I will reimburse you?"

Anji balked. "Hey, I don't want to be stuck for this."

"You won't," he assured her. "As soon as we're leaving, I'll pay the cash."

"What if we order room service and it's not on the bill and they come after me later? Y'know, it's hard to get a good credit rating when the bulk of your income is prize money."

"We won't order room service."

"What? You're not going to buy me lunch? A healthy diet is crucial."

"Fine. If we order room service, when it comes I will pay you the exact cash amount at the time. How's that?"

"What about the honor bar? Sometimes you take a water and it's complimentary and other times they want four dollars . . ."

Charles promised to pay for lunch, the honor bar, on-demand movies, he'd buy her the bathrobe in the room, whatever she wanted.

Anji mulled it over, then finally consented. Charles let out a silent sigh of relief.

He crossed back to the reception desk thinking, *It can't be this hard to have an affair.* He informed the non-pro that they'd be using Anji's card. She handed it to the clerk and his eyes lit up. "Anji De-Velera? Were you in the Ms. Fitness America contest?"

Oh, brother. Charles couldn't believe this.

The clerk was ecstatic. He had watched the event on ESPN2. He asked Anji if he could round up some of the guys and take a few photos.

"Look, we're on a very tight schedule," Charles interjected.

"Actually, you're not," said the clerk. "Your room isn't ready yet."

The Courtyard by Marriott in San fucking Bernardino was fully occupied? On a Wednesday? Whose bucket list includes *See the first McDonald's?*

For the next fifteen minutes Anji took pictures with every non-pro on the Courtyard staff. So much for discretion. Charles sat in a wicker chair in the corner of the lobby behind a plant, fuming and checking email. Apparently the two stars of *Blue Justice* wanted to do a scene where they showered together. Charles typed *NO!!!!* and hit send.

To occupy his mind he wondered if there had ever been television shows worth killing someone over. *All in the Family? M*A*S*H? Firefly* fans would probably sacrifice one of their own for another season. Still, it was hard to justify on cultural grounds. The world has somehow muddled on without more *Freaks and Geeks*.

A young family stepped out of the elevator. The mother, father, and sweet little cherub between them holding hands were practically skipping through the lobby—everyone was that happy and in love. Adulterer Charles could almost *feel* his hair turning gray.

Finally, after twenty photos of Anji had been taken, emailed to friends, and posted on Facebook and Twitter accounts, the love nest was ready.

"Do you need help with the luggage?" the desk clerk asked wryly.

"What do *you* think?" Charles growled.

At twelve thirty the ABN entertainment czar and Ms. Fitness finalist stepped off the elevator onto the third floor and found their room, conveniently located near the grinding ice machine. The room was sterile and functional. There was a king-sized bed and bathroom, which was all that was required. Charles crossed to the window, separated the curtains, and gazed out upon a field of oil pumps.

"The fantasy continues to play out," he muttered to himself and closed the curtains.

Anji sidled up to him, draped her sinewy tan arms around his shoulders, and kissed him. How long had it been since he'd kissed another woman? He decided that while his tongue was in her mouth he'd put a moratorium on that kind of thinking.

"Still a little nervous?" she asked, knowing the answer. Charles admitted there were a lot of things going on in his head. Then he looked into her eyes and was once again struck by her beauty. Had he ever been with a girl this exquisite? Certainly not in high school. There was that Swedish girl in college, but she had that scar on her leg and—again, stop! This was not the time to do a roll call. This was not the time to think about anything other than the here and now.

"You're very beautiful," Charles whispered. Anji put her finger to his lips. She offered to give him a massage.

"We're going to have some fun."

She poured the contents of her small purse onto the dresser. Among the items were massage oil, condoms, a Health Warrior chia seed bar, and a Hello Kitty wallet.

"I just don't know if—"

"Shhhhh. Don't talk. Just take off your clothes and lie on the bed."

Charles did as he was told. He removed his suit, hung it neatly in the closet, stripped down completely, and returned to the bed. Anji was waiting for him, completely naked.

"Oh . . . my . . . God," he whispered breathlessly. "I had never seen anything more utterly spectacular than the Iguazú waterfalls in Brazil. Until now . . . until your Brazil."

"Thanks. It hurt like a bitch to do, but I think it makes me look younger."

"The point is—I celebrate you."

"Yeah, I can see that. Boing."

The hell with the massage. Charles swept her into his arms. There is always that charge of electricity when two cool naked bodies first come together and touch. He pressed his mouth to hers and kissed her. There was no going back now.

Five minutes later they were in bed making hot, passionate love. Anji was on top of Charles, straddling, grinding, whipping him into an absolute frenzy. Her full natural breasts swayed, her blond hair swung from side to side. Charles thrust himself into her again and again. Anji moaned. Charles expressed himself the way he always expressed himself.

"Oh yes! This is exactly what I need! The hell with ratings, the hell with demographics, and sets-in-use! The hell with Gersh and Armantrout and Jantzen! I'm me! And you're me! And together we are celebrating . . . us! I have found my answer!"

****

The postcoital glow lasted until Colton, as Charles drove home in bumper-to-bumper traffic on the westbound San Bernardino Freeway. "You're my shrink!" he whined into the dashboard speakerphone. "You're my ethical adviser! How could you tell me to do that? I have just destroyed the foundation of my marriage!"

Dr. Gold tried to get a word in edgewise, but it was impossible. "Oh God," Charles continued. "What have I done? Trust . . . responsibility . . . I've destroyed it all! How will I ever look my wife in the face again?"

"Charles, take a breath—"

"How many murderers on their way to death row say, 'If only I had an affair I wouldn't be here'? None! That never comes up!"

"Okay. Settle down—"

"How will I ever look at my daughter? Goddamn that Gersh!"

"Come in. We'll talk about it."

"No. I can't come in now. I've got to get home. I've got to see my family. I told them this morning I was going to be in screenings all day. Now I have to make up three shows that I'm supposed to have seen!"

The Chevy Volt ahead of him slammed on its brakes and Charles, preoccupied, crashed into it. Without missing a beat, he added, "And now I have to explain why I got in an accident in West Covina!"

CHAPTER 8

CHARLES WAS VERY SUBDUED that night. Not that he was Robin Williams on Red Bull normally, but Sondra could definitely sense something was amiss. She prepared his favorite Cornish game hen and he didn't *celebrate* it. After picking at his dinner, he excused himself, claimed he was very tired, and slipped up to the guest room, where he crawled into his tiny twin bed and tried unsuccessfully to sleep.

His mind was a blur. Did Sondra suspect? She seemed to eye him warily. Women know. They just seem to have this sixth sense. He forgot who told him this—either one of his frat buddies or an FCC commissioner—but someone said, "No matter how many times you shower, they can still smell poontang on you." Of course, if Sondra went ballistic he couldn't blame her. He'd cheated on her . . . and worse, loved the shit out of it. Could he just put this day out of his consciousness and turn the page? Like he did when *ABN News with Ryan Seacrest* blew up in his face? Could he just pass the blame to Dr. Gold the way he did to the sports division when Ryan Seacrest did a less than stellar job calling the play-by-play for the Rose Bowl? Or would this be like Edgar Allen Poe's *Tell-Tale Heart*, where the drumbeat of guilt would continually beat and beat and beat in his ears until eventually he went completely mad? Was there a contemporary reboot of that classic that might make a good Halloween event movie of the week? Could he get a decent loaner while the Jag was in the shop?

As one o'clock rolled around Charles remained awake. He lay

motionless on the bed, remote in hand, channel surfing through the thousand-channel universe. Nothing interested him. He just stared at the flickering screen and ever-changing images, never changing expression—a zombie.

****

One oh-five a.m. and Sondra was still wide-awake, wondering what the hell was going on with her husband. "Screw it." She swung out of bed, walked down the hall, tapped on the door, and peeked in. There was the love of her life watching *Say Yes to the Dress*. She didn't even bother asking if he was okay. She knew he'd lie. Network presidents will never *not* say they're okay. What she loved about Charles was that among the network presidents, he was the only one who at least *knew* he was lying.

Sondra sat on the bed next to her troubled spouse. She gently took the remote out of his clammy hand as he continued to stare at the screen. *At least blink,* she thought.

To get his attention she tapped him on the shoulder. He finally noticed her presence. She had been in the room three minutes already.

"What is going on, Charles?" she asked with genuine concern.

"Nothing. What makes you think there's something wrong?" he answered.

"You looked absolutely horrible when you walked in tonight. I hardly recognized you. I hate that damn job of yours."

"The job? Oh. Yes, this job is unforgiving in its demands."

"It's a stern mistress."

"A stern *what?*"

"Charles, you're glowing red. Do you have a fever?"

****

Was she toying with him? Charles wondered. She let him off the hook with the job remark but came right back with that mistress crack.

She knew. She had to know. She was clearly sending a cryptic message. His life was over. His daughter would never speak to him again. He'd wind up one of those sad, broken men living in the Oakwood Garden Apartments in Burbank making himself dinners on a George Foreman grill. On the other hand, cryptic was not Sondra's style. Or maybe it was and he'd just never seen that side of her before. She'd never been suspicious before. She'd never had *cause* to be suspicious before. Oh Christ! Those flimsy drywalls in the Oakwood. At night you hear PornHub.com coming from four different units. But why would she take such a nurturing posture only to deliver a veiled bombshell? *Stern mistress* was just an expression. It was likely that it was just an innocent remark. Or at least an eighty-five percent chance that it was. Well . . . maybe seventy percent. Still, he liked those odds. He was probably okay.

But one thing was for sure. He did not have the temperament for illicit affairs. To risk everything for the sake of sex was insane. In fact, at that moment, the mere thought of sex was repellent. Besides, if the male body produced eighty-five million sperm cells daily, at this moment Charles had maybe six.

"I know I'll never break that obsession you have with being number one," she said softly. "But at least we can make love and I can give you something that no one else is able to give you. And it's been too long."

She put her arm around him. He let out a little whimper, trying not to cry.

"Charles?" she said, sounding surprised.

"No, no. I'm okay," he lied network presidentially.

She considered a moment, then said, "Maybe tonight's not a good night, honey."

She held him and stroked his hair, the way she would a child. Her compassion only made him feel worse.

"Sweetheart . . . ," she said.

"Yes?"

"You'd tell me if you were having a complete mental breakdown, wouldn't you?"

"Yes."

"All couples keep little secrets from one another, but that should-n't be one of them."

"No, I suppose it shouldn't."

He mustered a tiny smile. He imagined Hillary and Bill Clinton having this same conversation. Jack and Jackie too. Probably once a month. And he should be okay because part of Jaguar's service was that they supplied late-model loaners.

CHAPTER 9

THE POWER LUNCH IS a longtime Hollywood ritual. Whom you're seen with determines who you are. Generally these command performances were held in only two or three primary locations. Think of a bird migration, but instead of swallows substitute agents For years the Polo Lounge patio with its warm pastel colors in the prestigious Beverly Hills Hotel was the midday nest of choice. Then Le Dome on the Sunset Strip. For the last twenty years it's been the Grill on the Alley in Beverly Hills, where salmon and clients are both poached daily. And of course the Palm in West Hollywood. If you're important enough, there's a caricature of you on the wall.

That's where Charles Muncie sat in a dark wooden booth across from Frank Brunner, directly under Brunner's caricature. Yes, Charles had one too, but it was tucked away in the corner and smaller than the Real Don Steele's (a local disc jockey from the sixties)—a fact that did not go unnoticed by Mr. Muncie . . . or the widow of the Real Don Steele.

Frank Brunner's caricature was prominent, as well it should have been. For years he had been the president of ABN. Under his leadership the network dominated prime-time ratings for more than a decade. Known as the Silver Fox, even at seventy-five he remained news-anchor handsome.

Charles opened the conversation. "I can't tell you how good it is to see you again. You're my touchstone. I must tell you, I celebrate that."

"Right," said Frank, nodding thanks to the non-pro for bringing him his usual drink.

What followed was ten minutes of catching up—how's the family? When's your wife's charity? The Lakers need a power forward. That sort of shit.

The charming chitchat was interrupted by Charles' cell phone. The caller ID was blocked. Charles took the call anyway. What Frank heard was, "Hello? . . . Please. This is not a good time to call. Yes, I had a wonderful time too . . . Really, I'm in the middle of something. Let me get back to you."

He hung up the phone, hiding his embarrassment.

"Chippie on the side, Charles?" Frank asked.

"No, no," Charles scoffed. "That was . . . a writer I had a meeting with yesterday."

"You talk like that to a writer?"

"Well . . . she's a really good writer."

Frank chuckled. "Maybe you *should* get a chippie. You look like hell."

Charles good-naturedly dismissed that. "Pressures of the job. You know what that's like. You were ABN president for twelve years."

"Thirteen," Frank corrected.

Whatever. That was the *in* Charles needed. "I never actually talked to you about the end. It must have really been a feeling of satisfaction and relief when you stepped down, right?" he asked hopefully.

Frank sipped his vodka gimlet. "For all intents and purposes, when I walked out that door, my life ended."

Charles' heart sank.

"Sure, you spend the first couple of months on vacation and the 'more time with the family' routine. That gets old quick. I had my production deal, but I didn't know what I was doing. David Caruso in a comedy? What the fuck was I thinking?"

"Hey, I bought it."

"Then you look around for what to do next. You start really missing the action. Trouble is, how many jobs are there for *president?*"

Charles smiled gamely. He was so sorry he'd asked. Frank took a sip, then a swig. The floodgates had opened. "So you wind up as head of this fly-by-night and then that fly-by-night. You try to turn some fly-fishing channel into something normal people might watch. Eventually even that goes away. You become a legend, an icon, a *touchstone*. They cart you out to speak at the Museum of Broadcasting. Shit, I've got my own parking space there now. If I had to do it over again, I'd have done *anything* to hold on to that chair."

The word *anything* rang in Charles' ears. If Frank were in his place, would he kill Lucy Adamson to keep his job? Hell, he would kill Lucy Adamson to keep his caricature.

"Are you thinking of leaving?" Frank asked then.

"Me? Oh no. This job's my life," answered Charles, still with his forced smile.

Something caught Charles' eye and his mood turned dark. "Son of a bitch!" he growled under his breath.

Frank turned to see the object of Charles' scorn. Stevie Gersh had entered the room along with Fox president Marc Jantzen. The two were laughing and joking as they were shown a prime table by the window.

"*American Idol.*"

"What?" Charles said.

"*American* fucking *Idol*. I was set to buy that show but Fox swooped in and took it away. They're bastards."

"The lowest of the low."

Frank took a big sip and stared off into space. "God, how my life would have been different had we gotten *American Idol.*"

For the first time, Charles actually started to waver. There was his archrival, right in his face, practically daring him to take action. And it was pretty clear that his idol and mentor would have killed for Paula Abdul.

****

Charles paid the non-pro the seven dollars for parking his loaner car three steps from the restaurant and roared down Santa Monica

Boulevard heading east. Steam was still coming out of his ears. That fucking Jantzen was making a play. The only thing worse than *Gersh* going off the air was *Gersh* staying on the air but on Fox. Charles loathed Fox anyway. Besides *American Idol* there was *Fox News* and Marc Jantzen, and how many World Series broadcasts had they ruined by doggedly trotting out that windbag Tim McCarver?

Then there was Stevie Gersh—conniving, vengeful, and, ratings aside, not as funny as Louis C.K. on his worst day (also a member of the Fox/FX stable).

And finally, for good measure—what the fuck was Anji thinking, calling him? He'd sent her headshots to casting, paid for her gas, arranged for tickets to see *The Price Is Right*. What the hell did she want?

The light turned red at La Cienega and he eased the Infinity loaner to a stop. Two gay men crossed the street hand in hand. West Hollywood was nicknamed "Boys Town." It was pretty much the gay conclave of Los Angeles. Watching these two lovebirds in matching bicycle pants, Charles got an idea. He called his assistant, Lana, and told her there was a change of plans for the afternoon. He was going over to the Sony lot to talk with Neal Luder, the writer in charge of *Blue Justice*. Charles swung into the right lane and headed south to Culver City.

The Sony lot used to be the old MGM Studios back in the glory days of Hollywood. Clark Gable, Spencer Tracy, Kate Hepburn, Cary Grant, Greta Garbo, William Holden, crazy Joan Crawford, pre-crazy Judy Garland—these were fixtures at this legendary dream factory in the thirties and forties. Today *Wheel of Fortune* tapes there.

And also *Blue Justice*. Charles called Neal Luder's office en route and was told Neal was on the set. So Charles headed for Stage 16, where *The Wizard of Oz* and *That's My Bush* were once filmed.

He made his way through the maze of standing sets for *Blue Justice*—the police station, captain's office, neighborhood watering hole—and finally found cast and crew congregated around the apartment set. Thirty or forty technicians were scurrying about, adjusting overhead lights, fiddling with the camera, and swinging boom microphones. Neal Luder, the creator of the show and man in charge (known in the industry as the *showrunner*) sat off to the side in a director's chair. Neal was forty-seven and balding, had more circles under his eyes than a raccoon, and was just scraggly enough to be stopped at every TSA checkpoint. He was a longtime veteran of the TV wars. At one time he had hoped to become the next David Chase and create *The Sopranos*. But his career got bogged down writing procedurals (he used to joke that every show he worked on was called *initials:city*), and when he finally did break through with his own show, it was not a critical darling but became a moderate hit, and he decided that was way better. Depending on your choice of words, Neal Luder went through life either bemused or stoned.

Charles joined him and pulled up another director's chair. From above a loud bell rang. "Film is up," an echoed voice barked. Time to shoot a scene. All talking and movement ceased. From the loudspeaker came another voice proclaiming, "We have sound!" A crewmember stepped in front of the camera with a slate board and clapper sticks. He announced, "Scene eighteen, take four!" then clapped the sticks together loudly and deftly stepped aside. The director behind a video monitor offstage yelled, "Here we go. Everybody settle. Ready? And . . . action!"

The two stars of the show were in their no-frills New York apartment kitchen, cooking a gourmet meal. This was their dialogue as they sautéed and prepared garnish:

ESCALANTE: I don't care if Internal Affairs is on my ass. There's two bodies lying out there with their hands cut off. I'm not gonna be the good boy.
CHULSKY: You've got to let it go, hon.
ESCALANTE: You didn't see them! You didn't see the look on their faces! Their mouths and eyes wide open! Blood gushing from their severed limbs!
CHULSKY: You've got to hold on.
ESCALANTE: (screaming) Don't tell me to hold on!
CHULSKY: Come on, sit down. I made you those little empanada treats you like.

The director yelled, "Cut!" The bell sounded again, and six makeup people swarmed onto the set to do touch-up no one would ever notice.

Neal turned to Charles and said, "Y'know, time was I used to produce a *cop* show."

Charles tried to put a good spin on it. "Come on, Neal. My gut tells me this will open the show up to women."

Neal nodded. "Yes. That's what America wants to see—cops by day, marys by night. So what do you network folks want now? Want me to put in a musical number? Maybe attract some of the *Glee* crowd?"

Charles broke into his patronizing laugh, then responded. "What I do really think the show needs is a little more authenticity."

"What do you mean? We show a *tossed salad*? I was saving that for February sweeps."

Charles pressed on. "Neal, you've been doing this for so long, and you have such a treasure trove of knowledge. Lead us through this world we normally would never see."

Neal looked confused.

"Case in point—let's say someone wanted to . . . I don't know, random thought . . . hire a hit man. Who is this person? How would he be contacted?"

"You've seen us do that before."

"No. In detail," Charles reiterated. "Let's say that you, Neal Luder, wanted to hire a hit man. In real life. What would you do? Walk me through it."

Neal shrugged and started to answer but was interrupted by Charles' cell phone. Charles cursed the bad timing and answered the call. "Hello? . . . Oh, for godsakes."

He turned away from Neal. "I told you not to call this number . . . No. I can't . . . I'm pulling back from *what*? I told you who to call in casting, didn't I? I'm in the middle of a meeting. I'll call you tomorrow."

He disengaged the call and tried to mask his rage.

"Got a gumar on the side, Charles?" Neal asked, even more bemused than usual.

"You know me better than that."

"Uh-huh. If you say so."

"So anyway, about this hypothetical but real hit man. I contend that the audience is fascinated with crime—the *details* of it."

Neal took the bait. "Well, for something like this, there's a guy I know . . . Tony Zajak. He's the headwaiter at Matteo's. Used to be involved. I'd call him. He'd probably put me in touch with somebody who'd put me in touch with somebody. Don't make me use Ryan Seacrest as a guest star or I'm calling him."

That was worthy of patronizing laugh number two, almost a full-out chortle. Charles was pleased. That was the information he wanted. So now it was time to cover his tracks and leave. "Come to think of it, you're right. There have been a lot of hit-men episodes. But still, go back to that kind of authenticity."

"Well, great," Neal said. "Again you've saved the show."

Charles stood; they shook hands and exchanged good-byes. They confirmed that they'd see each other Saturday night for the big awards dinner.

"It will be nice to see Sondra again. Unless, of course, you're . . . y'know, bringing . . . someone else."

"There's no one else! And I'm not bringing her," said a flustered Charles. "I mean, I'm bringing my wife."

"Great. Well, see you there."

Neal chuckled wryly.

"What?"

"The Gay and Lesbian Coalition is honoring me. If only they knew how much I hate my fucking show."

CHAPTER 10

SONDRA COULDN'T UNDERSTAND why it was so important to Charles that the whole family attend the Lakers game three nights later. She was a little tired, it was a school night, and Kelly Rose wasn't used to being out so late. Plus the network had season tickets. They could have gone to any game. Why was this one so special? It was just against the Minnesota Timberwolves. Who gave a shit? But Charles was insistent. It had been a long time since the family just went out for a fun evening, and this was as good a night as any.

At one time the Dodgers were the Los Angeles team of choice. But they hadn't won a World Series since 1988. So now, to use Hollywood vernacular, they were in *sports franchise jail*. This was a town of front-runners and success. Failure was not tolerated. So when a big director put out two or three bombs in a row, he entered *director jail*, meaning no one would green-light his next movie. How does he escape director jail? By making a sleeper independent movie or getting an Emmy for directing an episode of *Orange Is the New Black*.

So the Lakers were LA's current darlings. There were also the Clippers, and in many ways they had the better NBA team, but they didn't have the glitz or championship banners. Jack Nicholson went to Lakers games. Billy Crystal went to Clippers games. 'Nuff said.

The Staples Center, home of the Lakers (and Clippers but mostly the Lakers), was divided into three main areas. There was a lower seating bowl right off the floor. This was where all the celebrities and industry types sat. Above that were three stories of luxury boxes that ringed the entire arena. These were the sole reason the venue existed. And finally, another seating section way above the timberline, a thousand miles from the action. This was where the actual fans were stowed.

Charles and his family sat in the lower level. He preferred that to the suites. Much easier to schmooze and be seen. What was the point of going to a Lakers game if you were just going to watch the game? The ABN seats were in section 119, looking straight at the foul line. Not as good as Denzel's, better than Stallone's.

The game started and Charles spent most of the time checking the clock—not the game clock or the twenty-four-second clock but the time-of-day clock just below the rafters. As usual, Sondra observed that he seemed distracted. This was becoming his normal state. And it was really starting to concern her because even leisure-time activities now appeared to give him no relief.

At 8:05 he turned to his wife. "I think I'm going to go up for a hot dog."

"Why? They have waiter service here." Waiter service was as much a precaution as a convenience. God forbid someone cut in front of Charlie Sheen in a beer line. Two concession stands and three condiments islands would be trashed.

"Still. I'd like to stretch my legs," Charles said.

He made his way up the aisle, waving at some asshole agent along the way, and disappeared into the concourse.

Once alone he took a deep breath, checked his watch, and proceeded to the escalators. Up he went. Level after level. Past the three stories of luxury suites. All the way up to the top.

People of color who weren't Oscar winners or former heavyweight boxing champions were in this section. Also Latinos and folks who wore Lakers jerseys and caps and cheered when their team scored a basket. Charles pulled out a little slip of paper: *8:10, section 322, top row, second seat in.*

Charles located the correct aisle and hiked up the stairs. The last row was empty. He sat in the designated seat. The players were ants, and yet the boisterous crowd was yelling, "Foul! He clipped him on the arm!" How the hell did they see the court, much less a ticky-tack foul?

Eight ten passed. Then 8:15. Charles was starting to get very nervous. Why was he even doing this in the first place? So far every step had been an exasperating experience. Charles met up with the headwaiter at Matteo's, dropped Neal Luder's name, and cryptically said he needed "something *fixed*." He was slipped a number after Charles slipped him a fifty. He called the number only to learn it was for a home repairman. Charles went back and said, "No, you misconstrued. I am looking for someone to *eliminate a problem*." This time his fifty dollars led him to a pest exterminator. On his third visit he flat-out said, "I need to take a contract out on someone's life. Do you know anyone who kills people for money?" This required a hundred dollars and Charles' buying the handsome coffee table book detailing Matteo's rich history since being established way back in 1963. There were pictures of Frank Sinatra on every page.

At 8:17 a nondescript man in his forties wearing an LA Kings hockey jersey and clutching a bag of popcorn trudged up the aisle and took a seat next to Charles.

"Charles, right?" he said.

"Yes."

This person might've been in one of those photos with Sinatra. It was hard to tell.

"All right, Charles, talk to me."

Wow. That was brusque. Charles was used to pleasantries. But he was clearly on this man's turf, not his, so he accommodated the gentleman and got right to it. First order of business: confirmation.

"So you're really a . . . ?"

"Don't finish that sentence," the man warned.

"You'll have to excuse me. The last lead I had turned out to be Mr. Bug-Droppings."

The hit man was getting a little annoyed. It wasn't like he had a notarized gun-for-hire license to show prospective clients. Or glowing testimonials on Yelp. "So what do you want already?"

"What do I say?" Charles hoped the hit man would have a little compassion. This was all very new and terrifying to him.

Making Charles feel comfortable was not something the hit man concerned himself with. "Tell me what you need; then we'll fill in the details. The white kid's lucky he didn't get called for that little stutter step right there."

"You saw that?"

"It's not like he doesn't stick out."

Charles took another deep breath. This was like an out-of-body experience. He couldn't believe he heard himself say, "It's a woman. Her name is Lucy Adamson."

"Stevie Gersh's girlfriend?"

Swell. A hit man who watched *TMZ*. This was just too weird. Charles started to get up, but his seatmate pulled him back down. "Sit for a moment."

Charles collected himself. "You see—"

The hit man held up his hand. "I don't give a shit. We're talking about a public figure here."

"No, she's not. She's a non-pro."

"There will be major headlines. This will cost you a great deal of money. A half a million and I won't even say that's final."

Charles was flabbergasted. "Half a million? For a non-pro? This has got to come out of my own pocket."

"Take out a student loan," the hit man said with a shrug.

"I was planning maybe a hundred thousand, which is a whole lot of money, even today."

"For a hundred thousand I'd kill one of those refs. Hell, I'd kill 'em all." Charles gasped. The hit man chuckled. "I'm just kidding with ya. But unlike these guys, she'd be *missed*."

Charles just sat there, completely stunned. The hit man could see this was going nowhere. He told Charles that if he couldn't come up with that kind of cake they had nothing to talk about and he started to rise.

"Wait!"

Charles gestured to please sit back down. It was time to utilize his particular skills. "All right, let me propose something—a chance to make much more than just half a million," he said, turning on the charm. "What if we waive the five hundred thousand dollars and I give you a production deal at ABN?"

"What?!"

Charles laid out the scenario. "Set you up in your own company. Give you a commitment for a show on the air. I'll put you with a writer/producer."

"Well, what would *I* do, then?" the hit man wondered.

Charles smiled broadly. "You won't have to do anything."

The hit man sat back in his seat and munched on a handful of popcorn. Charles was mildly encouraged. The hit man was actually considering it. After a moment the hit man replied. "Could I star in it?"

Now it was Charles who said, "What?!"

"Why do you think I got into this? I'm an actor. I needed a job that was flexible, so I could go on auditions."

Charles asked him if he was any good. After all, stars of network shows generally have more on their résumés than just expert marksmanship.

"My reel's up on YouTube. Decide for yourself. I also have a commercial reel. I'm the stay-at-home dad who bakes the Duncan Hines cakes."

"Okay, this sounds promising. And what name do you use?"

"My stage name is Robert McManus. Bobby when I do comedy."

Charles was about to ask him his credits when his cell phone chirped. He saw who it was, then stuffed the phone in his pocket.

"A girl?" guessed Robert.

"I don't wish to discuss it."

"Oooh, *now* who's being all secretive and mysterious?"

"I need the job done within three weeks."

Robert stroked his chin, considered, and then finally said, "Okay. But I want promotion. And I don't want my show to be buried on Friday night."

The out-of-body experience continued, because surely the *real* Charles Muncie didn't say, "Fine. You've got a deal."

****

The Muncies left the game early. Kelly Rose was falling asleep, Sondra was bored, and Charles was in a fog following his return from "the concession stand." To avoid the construction slowdown on the westbound Santa Monica Freeway, Charles headed home via surface streets. Olympic Boulevard generally flew once you got past Koreatown.

Charles was completely silent. His hands held the wheel in a death grip and he stared straight ahead with a tight-lipped, pained expression. By the time they had reached La Brea, Sondra had had enough.

"Charles, I just can't stand this," she blurted out.

"I'm sorry. I don't mean to do that," he answered, almost by rote.

"So what is it tonight? Maybe I can help."

Charles, as usual, said it was nothing.

Sondra tried to reason with him, put things in perspective. "You're right. It *is* nothing. It's just television. And I bet if you step back for a moment and look at your real life, you'd be surprised how problem-free the whole damn thing is."

Charles had no answer. He stopped at the light at Fairfax. He glanced to his left. A red Camry pulled up next to him. Inside was Anji. She turned to Charles and glared at him for avoiding her. Startled, he hit the gas and peeled out before the light had turned green. Sondra went batshit. What the hell was going on? And how much longer could she stand this craziness?

CHAPTER 11

EVEN ATTEMPTING TO GET some sleep that night was futile for Charles Muncie. So instead, he sat zombielike in his darkened study in his darkened house and watched television. But only one. Six were switched off and the one that remained was tuned to a religious program hosted by a toupeed televangelist and his overly made-up scary wife.

"It doesn't matter what you've done, what sins you've committed," said the woman who looked like a cross between Dolly Parton and the Joker. "Even the blackest heart can be filled with the light of goodness and righteousness. But you need His help."

"Amen," mouthed Charles.

The husband with the dead squirrel on his head picked it up from there. "You need Jesus Christ as your personal savior and you need Him today. Call one of these numbers now and there will be somebody there to talk with you, to pray with you, to help you find everlasting peace. Go ahead."

Charles picked up the phone. He was so desperate he was willing to try even *this*. A soothing voice answered. Charles responded, "Hello . . . I'd like to pledge a thousand dollars. Could you pray for me?"

"Praise Jesus! Of course," the appreciative voice cooed. "What is your name?"

"Jim Phelps."

****

The Beverly Hilton Hotel has stood for fifty years on the western border of Beverly Hills. Its International Ballroom has been the site of many Hollywood events. It was where music chieftain Clive Davis held a big bash three hours after his longtime client Whitney Houston was found dead in one of the upstairs rooms. At one time owned by TV personality/game-show mogul Merv Griffin, the Beverly Hilton had for years been the site of the Golden Globe Awards, which meant that show business royalty from Sir Laurence Olivier to Pia Zadora have given acceptance speeches from its stage. Olivier won a Golden Globe that literally broke apart before the play-off music even began.

On this Saturday night the Gay and Lesbian Coalition was holding their annual awards dinner. The gala formal affair was packed. Dinner was mediocre, but what do you expect for a thousand dollars a plate? Charles was one of the speakers once the ceremonies began and everyone's half-eaten chicken plate had been cleared away.

"I believe as a network—and a network is a family—the time has come to stand up for diversity. To celebrate our differences. To welcome gays and lesbians into our shows, therefore into our homes. As the King of Kings, Jesus Christ, said, 'Suffer the little children to come unto me.' We are all His children, no matter who we are, no matter what we do, no matter how bad we are."

Sondra and Neal Luder listened from their table just off the stage.

"What the *fuck*?" Sondra said.

"When did Charles become a Jesus guy?" Neal said.

Sondra shook her head. "I've never heard him talk about religion in his life, ever . . . except to say it would kill a show in five minutes."

Charles finished his speech to polite applause and crossed right to the bar in the back of the ballroom. He ordered a vodka on the rocks. The bartender, a young man in his twenties who was either a writer or an actor said, "Great speech, Mr. Muncie. Praise the Lord."

"Yes. Praise Him. Can you just get me my fucking drink?"

Fox president Marc Jantzen bellied up to the bar. Of course he would be here. Marc ordered a scotch on the rocks and turned to his chief rival. "Wonderful words, Charles. Your speech was a big hit." Charles mustered a fake smile. Marc looked around at all the gays and lesbians in attendance. "If all else fails with ABN, you'll always have the one percent that these people represent," said Marc.

Charles was in no mood for banter. He finished the bar nuts he was munching and said, "You really think you're going to steal Stevie Gersh from me?"

"What? That lunch?" Marc said innocently. "We're just friends. Both big baseball fans."

"Oh yeah? What team is Miguel Cabrera on?" Charles asked.

"Come on, Charles. I don't know every player on every team."

"He won the Triple Crown in 2012. First man to do that in forty-five years!"

"Okay, Charles, you got me. We're both fans of *pussy*. Ask me a pussy question."

Charles did not find him amusing and said so. As if Marc cared. "If I were you, I'd watch my back," Marc warned, "because Gersh is very get-able. I mean, he called me."

Charles should have been surprised but wasn't. That's exactly the kind of thing Stevie Gersh would do. Especially to him. But this time Charles was unruffled. This time Charles had a plan. "I caution you, Marc," he said in a low, menacing tone, "do not underestimate me. I assure you, I have the ability to do whatever it takes."

Marc took that in stride and sipped his own drink, which had just arrived. "Knowing Gersch, he just might want you to get on your knees and give him a blow job."

Oh, if it were only that easy, Charles thought.

Marc spotted someone over Charles' shoulder.

"Uh-oh. Bimbo alert!"

Charles turned and almost did a spit take. There was the lovely Anji, wearing the shortest killer black dress allowed in polite society. She was circulating the room as if *looking for someone.*

"Incredible body, huh?" Marc said. "She was a Ms. Fitness finalist or something."

Charles knew he should leave and find someplace to hide—like

India—but his curiosity got the best of him.

"You know her?"

Marc leaned back against the bar on one elbow. "Sort of. She's fucked three of my development VPs. A classic gold digger looking for that big acting shot. "

Charles thought if there were a country of schmucks, he would be their king.

"She even came on to me at a pilot filming one night," Marc added.

Of course she did.

"And you weren't tempted?" Charles asked as casually as he could.

Marc laughed. "Tempted? Of course I was tempted. But give me some credit for brains, Charles. I'm a damned network president, for godsakes. I should be able to spot someone like her a mile away."

"Indeed. Yes. Of course." Charles would be the schmuck country's king for life.

Anji finally spotted him. Like a heat-seeking missile she marched up to the bar. It was too late for escape. "Why have you been avoiding me?" she barked to the president of ABN.

"Ohh-kay," chuckled his Fox counterpart, confirming what he'd suspected just by the nature of Charles' interest. "Well, I'll let you two kids gab. Have a superfun evening, both of you," Marc said, then walked away from the wreckage.

This situation was pushing Charles to the brink. He felt himself bleeding out of his eyes.

"Damn it, stop this!" he ordered at low volume.

"What am I supposed to do? You won't take my calls."

"I told you not to call."

"Don't eat those bar nuts. They're filled with salt. Horrible for you."

"Look, whatever happened that one time, it was one time only."

"That's not what you said that day."

"You can't hold a man to what he was saying when he was fucking! Monica Lewinsky would have been attorney general. Didn't I fulfill our obligation? Didn't I set you up with a casting director?"

"You used me."

Charles was apoplectic. "Me?" he said, still keeping his voice down to a rumble. "You used *me*. To get you on television. And you should have a banner career, because it seems I'm not the only one helping you."

"The others don't matter to me."

"Don't say that! Don't you say that!"

Anji changed her tone, now more tender. "But it's true."

"It's fictitious."

"Huh?"

"It's not true."

"It is. There's a goodness about you, Charles. And now I know that we're joined by our love for our Lord Jesus Christ."

"Oh God!"

"Praise His name," said the bartender.

"Praise Him," from Anji.

Charles just shook his head. This couldn't be happening. He reached for the beer nuts and she gently smacked his hand.

"So, Charles, I want you to know that I'm never going to let you go. If it takes weeks, if it takes months, even if it takes years . . ."

"Charles?" another voice chimed in.

He whirled around and let out an involuntary yelp. Sondra was approaching. He recovered quickly and greeted her warmly.

"You've been gone a long time," she said. "I thought maybe you had gone to confession."

"No, no. Just talking business."

There was the hot-looking elephant in the sleek black minidress in the room.

Charles introduced Anji, identifying her as a rising young producer. "We're talking to her about an exciting project we might get in bed with . . . uh, that we might *do* together."

"Right-o!" said Anji.

Sondra sized her up. There was something familiar about her. "Weren't you Ms. Fitness or something?"

Holy shit! Did *everyone* know who she was? It was like the two most recognized symbols on the planet earth were Mickey Mouse and Anji DeVelera.

"I finished third in Hawaii this year," a delighted Anji crowed.

"That's right. I've seen your picture in the gym. I go to Pro Gym in Brentwood."

Pro Gym was owned by Ryan O'Neal and frequented by numerous celebrities. The attraction was that it was very low-key. The notables could go about their workouts without being recognized or bothered—or in Ryan's case, arrested. Of course the celebrities also provided photos of themselves to be plastered on the walls. Stars never wanted to be *that* unrecognized.

"Oh yes. I used to be a trainer there."

Natch.

"Well, now she's a hot young producer. This is the one town where that kind of thing can happen," Charles interjected.

"Do you still do any training on the side?" Sondra asked. "Because I just lost my person."

"Sondra, she's a *producer*!" Charles reiterated. "Would you ask Jerry Bruckheimer to give you Spanish lessons?"

"Well, I don't train anymore." The Ms. Fitness runner-up shrugged. "But as a favor to Charles, I could, y'know, come over to your house."

He was ready to come out of his skin. Now his mistress was going to train his wife in his house? That had to cross a line. Probably six lines.

Sondra was thrilled and made a date for that Saturday.

Anji smiled devilishly at Charles and said cheerily, "We'll talk." Then she flitted off to be the eye candy of every man in the ballroom who wasn't gay—all nine of them.

At least Sondra didn't suspect, Charles thought, trying to put the best spin on things. Unless she *did* and this was a way to really get back at him. He immediately chased that terrifying notion from his head. *Think positively. Always think positively.* So what silver lining could he find from this granite cloud? Maybe this incident would make a great scene in one of his shows. It had never been done. Oh, wait. It had. A different version of this very scene. In *Slumdog Millionaire* when little Jamal had to jump into a pool of shit.

Sondra broke his train of thought by asking him to get her some wine. Charles said, "Of course," and she returned to the table. At least from the back she didn't need a trainer. He spun back to the bar and raised his empty glass. "White wine and a double of this."

The bartender nodded and muttered, "Even the Son of God ain't gonna save *your* ass."

Charles didn't hear him. He was too busy thinking and calculating. Was Anji doing this to get back at him or get closer to him? Was Sondra unaware or being vindictive? She had never been vindictive before. Except how would he know? Would Standards and Practices even allow a broadcast network to show the shit scene from *Slumdog Millionaire*? Did they film an alternative? What would that be?

Charles also didn't notice the attractive young brunette with a kind face and gentle smile who approached the bar and ordered a red wine. She, however, noticed him.

"Charles? Hi. Lucy Adamson. We met a couple of times on the set of *Gersh* and up at Stevie's house."

"Oh, of course," Charles said, snapping out of it and staring into the face of the very last person in the galaxy he wanted to see.

"I loved your speech. I didn't know you were religious."

"I try to keep it separate from my job," Charles replied, hoping the bartender would hurry up with his fucking order. How long did it take to pour a goddamn glass of white wine? If Jesus Christ had ordered it, it would have been up in a flash.

"I guess you heard I'm no longer with Stevie."

Charles nodded ruefully. Lucy felt the need to explain. "He's been going around saying it's because there was somebody else. But just so you hear the truth, that's not what it was. As you know, Stevie can be . . . very high maintenance. Like, a twenty-four-hour-a-day thing. I just didn't have the time. My mother's become quite sick."

"Oh, I'm sorry to hear that."

"Thank you. I'm really the only one there for her. I know a lot of people think I'm nuts, walking away from the most eligible man in America, but my mother and I have always been very close. More like friends. When I was a kid, I had spinal meningitis. She sat with me for the two years it took to recover. Even gave up her career. So how can I turn my back on her now?"

Charles nodded and swallowed the lump in this throat.

"Normally, I'm not one to get even, but I'm just so doggone mad about the hurtful, horrible things Stevie's been saying about me. I just needed to tell my side."

Again, a silent nod from Charles. He couldn't speak. His head was swimming. The ground began to shift. Here was maybe the sweetest, most noble creature he had ever had the privilege to meet, an absolute angel of mercy—and he'd arranged a hit out on her. Good luck pledging a thousand dollars for absolution on this one.

Their orders were up. Lucy took hers, thanked Charles for letting her vent, and told him to have a lovely evening. As she crossed back to her table, Charles watched and noted to himself that she *really* did-n't need a trainer. *God, what a lowlife I am,* he thought. *It's not enough I arrange to kill someone; I need to get a hard-on too?* He downed his vodka like it was a tequila shot. Signaling to the bartender that he wanted another, he ducked into the richly appointed foyer.

There was no way he could go through with this. Lucy Adamson deserved to be celebrated, not plugged between the eyes. He grabbed his iPhone to call Robert the hit man but stopped. Idiot! Cell phone calls were monitored. Obama was probably listening. And cell phone calls leave a paper trail. That's how Escalante and Chulsky got their man every other week on *Blue Justice*. Of course now they were too busy waxing each other to concentrate on evidence.

Stop it! Charles snapped at himself. Why did his mind have to be so active? Why was his consciousness constantly barraged with stray thoughts and questions? Why couldn't he just be like Lindsay Lohan and go through life completely thought-free? Was Lindsay Lohan the best example? Would Kim Kardashian be better? Damn it! There he went again. What was the original thought?

A pay phone. He had to get to a pay phone.

Were there even pay phones anymore?

Fortunately, in a large hotel like the Beverly Hilton there were. He left the ballroom and followed the thick-carpeted hallway to the lobby. And yes, off to the side by the front desk was a bank of pay phones. Charles wondered if newer hotels like the W still had pay phones. God, he hated it when he was under enormous stress and his mind raced. Paula Abdul was another good candidate for airhead. But was she dumb or just drugged-out on meds?

Charles picked up the receiver and glanced around to make sure no one was watching. He retrieved the number out of his wallet, dumped in every bit of change he had—who knew how much pay phone calls were these days?—and punched in the number.

It rang three times, then: "Hi, this is Robert McManus. I'm not home right now. But you could leave me a message or better yet, go to YouTube and check out my new commercial for Duncan Hines. Just type in 'Dad, can I lick the spoon?' Okay, I'll call you back. "

After the beep, Charles said, "Hello. This is the person you met at the Lakers game Tuesday night. I just want to say the deal is off. Repeat: the deal is off. The deal is definitely off. But in good faith I will still develop one project, although with an option, not a commitment. Again, to reiterate—the deal is O-F-F. Please confirm that you got this. But not on my cell phone. Email me. No, that's no good. Tell you what—text me from a phone other than your own and say 'Julia Roberts will consider doing a series.' That will be the code. Again: 'Julia Roberts will consider doing a series.' Thank you."

He hung up and, somewhat relieved, rested his head on the receiver. So he lost his job. Everything he ever worked for. Stepped down in disgrace. Even if he had to teach broadcasting at the DeVry Institute, at least he didn't take a human life. How insidiously corrupt was television and how morally bankrupt was he that he even took this inexcusable act this far? Charles started to collect himself and could feel the blood returning to his head. At least he'd done one good thing. He'd called off a murder.

His sense of satisfaction and relief was short-lived because as he checked the coin return for change, he spotted, out of the corner of his eye . . .

Robert McManus. Way on the other side of the lobby, looking natty in a tuxedo, and strolling into the ballroom.

Charles did a double take—a reaction so exaggerated no actual human being ever did one. He stiffly but quickly cut through the lobby. He tried to go as fast as possible without attracting any undue attention. The result was something between a walk and a run— more like a goose step.

Once inside the ballroom, his heart sank even further. The large room was packed now with folks mingling and couples dancing to the pounding DJ-provided music. Robert was not in view. He could've been anywhere.

Charles weaved his way through the dance floor. He darted around, frantically scanning faces, while "Smooth" by Carlos Santana blared.

Still no luck. Damn! Where was he? He could be up in the rafters somewhere by now. Or slipping something in Lucy's drink. Charles had thoughtlessly neglected to ask Robert what his assassination method of choice was.

He didn't see Robert, but he did spot Lucy alone at a table. She wasn't slumped over, so that was a good sign. Maybe he could get her out of there.

Charles goose-stepped quickly to her and asked for a dance.

"Then you're not mad at me for causing any problems with Stevie?" she said.

"Not at all. Please, join me," Charles answered, offering his hand.

Lucy took it and stood. "I'm so relieved. I thought you were going to kill me."

Charles laughed heartily, then practically yanked her out onto the floor. They began movin' and a-groovin'. Charles discreetly danced around her, hoping to cut off any good kill angle.

The song ended. "Thank you," Lucy said.

"How about another?"

Which turned into another and another and still another after that.

This did not go unnoticed by Sondra. She sat at her table with Neal Luder, steaming.

"That's the fourth dance in a row he's had with her."

"How you two doing?" Neal asked, knowing the answer based on this and the phone call Charles took on the set that day.

"Not good."

Neal drained the last of his scotch on the rocks. "Come on. Running a gay cop show, I've learned a step or two."

Sondra smiled. He took her hand and led her onto the floor. They began to dance not far from Charles and Lucy.

Neal tapped Charles on the shoulder. "Can I cut in?"

"I'd really rather . . . ," Charles said, then spotted Sondra with him. "Of course."

Neal took Charles' place with Lucy. Charles danced with his wife, all the while scanning the room for Robert.

"Still waiting for my drink," Sondra said.

"Oh Jesus. I'm sorry. The kid was out of white wine, had to go back to the storeroom for more, and . . ."

"Yeah, yeah. So who was that?"

"Huh? Oh. Lucy Adamson. Stevie Gersh's girl. It's been pretty tough on her. He's been saying a lot of derogatory things about her, and I just wanted to reassure her that I'm not one of those people who's going to shun her just because she's not going with Stevie anymore and thus no longer in the ABN family."

"Are you having something with her?"

"What? No. Of course not. Sondra, for godsakes! You're the only woman in my life."

"Then why can't you even look at me?"

"Sondy, I am not having an affair," Charles exclaimed with false conviction.

A hand tapped Sondra on the shoulder. "Can I cut in?"

It was Anji.

"Why not?" said Sondra, resigned.

Sondra drifted off as Anji took her place. "Who was the woman you were dancing with before?"

"Anji, do you want money? I have money."

"I'm not interested in money. Y'know, I went to a psychic yesterday who said I was going to get involved in a long-term relationship with a very powerful man who is already involved with someone. Now, tell me that's not you."

"That's every straight man in this room!"

"She meant you."

"Would you like your own show?"

"I'm a determined woman, Charles. You don't finish third in the Ms. Fitness America contest without being a very determined woman."

Finally! Charles spotted Robert slithering through the crowd.

"I've got to go."

She held him tight. "Where?"

"For godsakes, let me go!"

He wriggled free but immediately was grabbed by Sondra. "At least have the decency to finish the dance with your wife."

Shit! He dutifully rocked out for a few anxious beats. And it didn't help that the song was "Kill Everybody" by Skrillex. It finally ended . . . or at least there was a break in it. Charles seized the opportunity. "There. That was marvelous. I'll be right back."

He dashed off, leaving a confused Sondra alone on the dance floor.

Relieved, he spotted Robert—now in line at the bar.

"We have to talk," Charles whispered upon reaching him.

"Not here, idiot."

"Then where? This is important."

"Parking structure, level three, in five minutes."

"Fine."

Charles turned to leave, then turned back.

"What?"

"Where on level three?"

"I dunno. Near the elevator."

"Splendid. Thank you."

Charles started off but once again returned.

"Is there only one elevator? Sometimes in large structures there are ones on either—"

"I'll find you!"

"Okay. Perfect. But please don't kill anyone till then."

"Get the fuck away from me."

CHAPTER 12

THERE WAS ONLY ONE ELEVATOR on level three. And no parking spaces. Frustrated cars circled in vain. One Acura passed by four times. Charles was the first to arrive (of course). Five minutes turned into twelve. Shouldn't hit men be prompt?

Robert finally emerged out of the shadows. "So what do you want?" he asked without bothering to apologize for his tardiness.

Charles wasted no time. "You were going to whack her there in a crowded room?"

"No. I was here for the dinner. I'm a member of the coalition."

"You're gay? A gay hit man?"

Robert shrugged. "Hey, we kill too."

Charles just shook his head. "Listen," he said, "I want to call this off."

"Yeah, I figured. The guilt of taking another life is overwhelming. No way you can live with yourself after an act like that. It's something that will stay with you and eat away at your soul until the day you die."

"No, no," Charles said. "I just want to make a change. I want you to kill Anji DeVelera instead."

"What?"

The Acura approached again. Charles was silent until it passed. "Yes. Lucy Adamson I can't go through with. But the other woman is threatening my home, not my job. Both things are dear to me. But if I'm going to take a life, I want my priorities to be straight."

Now Robert shook his head. Things were always so much

cleaner when it was a government hit. He mulled over the change in plans for a moment, then made his decision.

"All right. Same deal. I still get my show."

"Your show was for a celebrity hit."

"What's her name again?"

"Anji DeVelera."

Robert's eyes lit up. "Anji De—from the Ms. Fitness America pageant?"

By now Charles was resigned to the fact that everyone in the universe knew who she was except him. "Yes. Finished third in Hawaii—"

"In my book that still qualifies as a celebrity. A lot of heartsick fanboys are going to be building shrines in their basements."

"All right. Same deal."

Emotionally spent, Charles leaned against a white Prius. The Acura came by again. "You leaving?" the driver called out.

"No."

"Then fuck you," the frustrated Acura owner said.

"No! Fuck you!" Charles yelled back. "Fuck you. And your fucking BMW-wannabe piece-of-shit Acura! They're not even as good as Saabs, you son of a bitch!"

Charles caught himself. Clearly, the frustration was getting to him. The composure that had always been at his disposal was beginning to desert him. That was a frightening prospect. Putting up a good front was pretty much his only gift.

He leaned back against the Prius and took a few long, calming breaths. Robert wisely gave him a wide berth during his little hissy fit. He waited for Charles to settle down, then approached.

"Listen, I came up with the show I want to do. I'm kind of a Civil War buff."

Charles glared at him. He was pitching a show? *Now?! Really?* Robert barreled on.

"They say write about what you know. I would play a plantation owner who's actually working for the Union. Every week, I capture a Confederate general or someone in the administration, bring them back north. The second half of the show is the trial."

"What are you talking about?" Charles blurted out. "No one ever did anything like that! What kind of Civil War buff are you?"

"Hey, I'm taking a little creative license. Like Tarantino. Putting my own distinctive stamp on history. It would be my *Django*."

"You are seriously comparing yourself to Quentin Tarantino?"

"I may not yet have his penchant for filmmaking, but I'd have to give the edge to myself when it comes to violence."

"I'll think about it."

"No, you won't."

"Come up with something else. But that reminds me, just how are you going to do it?"

"Single camera. Maybe handheld."

"No. The assassination."

"What about it?"

"What is it your method?"

Robert eyed him suspiciously. "Why?"

"I'm curious; that's all. It occurred to me you never divulged just how you were planning to accomplish this hit," Charles said.

"Well, let's see . . . First I use chloroform to knock her out. Then I drag her to an abandoned shed, and when she wakes up she's naked, tied to a table. The room is covered in plastic and I've assembled photos of all the people she's done wrong. That reminds me, I need a recent picture of you. Then I plunge a knife into her heart."

"Really? You've modeled your assassin career after *Dexter*? Y'-know, I passed on that show and now I'm glad. As a responsible broadcaster I can't allow sickos—or in your case, *professionals*—to get their lethal inspiration from my network."

"No, you moron. I shoot her. I take a gun and put a fucking bullet in her head."

"Oh. Right. Of course."

"Like they do on all of *your* shows."

"Okay. I didn't think I could feel worse than I did five minutes ago, but I was wrong. Thank you for that."

"Oh, get real. You can't feel responsible for every murder just because you air cop shows. You worry about that shit and it'll fucking eat you alive."

"No, it's not that. I'm kicking myself again for not picking up *Dexter.*"

Robert started off. "Just know it'll be done. Quick, clean, and noncinematic. And my Civil War idea is better than half the shit you have on your network."

Robert disappeared into the shadows. Charles required another moment before he could go back to the soiree. He needed to reconcile in his head—or just plain fool himself—that the truly heinous act he had just committed was even somewhat, on some obscure level, justified.

The Acura zipped around again and the driver yelled out at Charles, "Asshole!"

CHAPTER 13

Come, ye sinners, poor and needy,
Weak and wounded, sick and sore;
Jesus ready stands to save you,
Full of pity, love, and pow'r.

THAT WAS WHAT THE seven-member house choir of SaviorTV was singing on all six monitors in Charles' entertainment center. Charles kneeled before the screen, his hands in the prayer position, eyes closed, quietly singing along with the hymn.

As usual, his mind began to drift. What kind of ratings did this show get? Were they on in the middle of the night because the airtime was cheaper? Or had it been determined that those in need of spiritual guidance also tended to be sleep deprived? Does *believing* act almost like an Advil PM? How much do independent stations and cable networks charge these broadcast ministries? Do the Christian viewers who donate realize that a good portion of their dollar probably goes to Jews? Charles smiled at the irony.

What if ABN ran one of these salvation programs during the overnight? And would it be more prudent to just barter the time and let the ministries program it, or should ABN own the show outright and program it themselves? Might they make a bigger percentage of the cut? And they could give the preachers notes! There were parts of the presentation that lagged, Charles noticed. Notably the teaching segments. Seth Meyer's audience was too young, but Jesus Christ could easily take a bite out of Craig Ferguson.

Suddenly the sound went off. Charles' eyes flew open like window shades. He turned back. Sondra was standing over him, holding the remote in one hand, a glass of red wine in the other. She spoke in a measured tone.

"Y'know, some of my girlfriends tell me their husbands go down to their offices in the middle of the night, watch porno online, and jerk off. I envy those women."

"Sondra, I—"

"There was a mother in Kelly Rose's playgroup, I forget her name, who said she discovered her husband on his knees giving a blow job. I think I envy *her*."

Charles got up wobbling. "Look, I just can't stop watching these people. They seem so free. So unburdened."

"If you feel the need for God, let's go to church. I'd go to church. But this is not church. This is the Juiceman but he's selling God."

Charles was not in the mood to defend video soul saving. He told her he was fine and to go back to sleep.

"I know what's going on," she said, swirling her glass.

Game changer! That caught his attention. "Wha-what do you mean?" he asked cautiously.

"I know, you bastard."

"What?"

She took a step closer to him. He felt like backing up but decided not to. "The no sleeping, the drinking, the finding God. You've been keeping something from me and I'm furious about it."

Checkmate. Charles knew he was trapped. Nothing left to do now but confess. And maybe get down on his knees again. "Sondy, please, believe me when I say it had nothing to do with—"

She cut him off. "Stevie's not coming back next year, right?"

"What?" said Charles, thrown but massively relieved.

"I have to hear it from Marc Jantzen's wife? I don't hear it from my own husband? Are you sleeping with anybody? Or do I have to find that out by watching *TMZ*?"

"Okay, it's true."

"What?!"

"No, not the sleeping part!" he added before she could throw the wine in his face. "The *Stevie* part. At least it looks that way."

"And you're worried that the whole thing is going to come apart."

"Well . . . yes."

"Why didn't you tell me?"

He looked down at his feet, too sheepish to make eye contact. "I don't know. It's my training. Years of keeping the lid on bad news. Coming up with the right spin. Lying if need be. I didn't know how to tell you that I'd lose my job."

"You'd lose your job?"

Shit! She didn't know that either. "Very, very small chance," he blurted out again. "Microscopic. It's just my own paranoia, because they've expressed tremendous support."

Sondra took a long sip of her wine. "Why is he leaving?" she asked finally.

Charles took the glass from her and had a sip of his own. It was a Chablis but he imagined it was the blood of Jesus. "I don't know for sure. Somehow it's all tied up with Lucy Adamson. She rejected him. For him to be rejected, I think he's gone slightly out of his mind. Actors! They're the devil, Sondra. All of them. Satan doesn't have a pitchfork and a tail. He has an Emmy and two hundred thousand Twitter followers!" Charles took another sip and silently said, *Praise Jesus*, then, *Very light, very floral.*

"Well, what are you going to do about this?"

"What can I do? He's certifiable. I've offered him the world. God, if only Lexapro were available in suppository form!"

"Have you thought about introducing him to someone else?"

"What good is that going to do?" Charles scoffed, realizing he had never thought of that himself.

"It could do all the good in the world," said Sondra. "He's not interested in more money. He's interested in acceptance, validation, love. Be his friend. Do *the guy* thing. Fix him up with someone cute. Insist that he meet her."

"I don't think you're grasping how hurt he is. He's on a whole other echelon of hurt." A thought occurred to him. What if Amy Grant hosted the overnight God show?

"You want to keep your job? Fight for it. All I see is you sitting here waiting for an answer from people with bad hair."

"This is a very complicated and delicate matter."

"Bullshit!" Sondra's eyes lit up. "Oh. You know who would be perfect? That Anji who's going to come over here Saturday."

Charles' head almost exploded. "No. I don't really see those two together in any—"

"Are you crazy?" Sondra said, getting more excited. "She's gorgeous. You've seen the body on her. And you know what a letch Stevie is. For her part, I'd bet she'd hop into bed with any buffoon who looked the least bit needy."

"Sondy, I don't think this is a productive solution," said Charles, beads of sweat forming on his brow.

"Charles, for once, would you not think of me as just your *sanctuary* and shut me out? Let me help you. I'll call Stevie and invite him over Saturday for tennis." He was about to protest when she cut him off. "Charles, I'm doing it. Come on. Come to bed."

She draped her arm around him and led her resigned husband out of the office. Once they got to the end of the hallway, she peeled off into the master bedroom and he crossed to the guest room bathroom, where he threw up and made a mental note to go online and check out recent photos of Amy Grant to see whether guys would still want to fuck her.

CHAPTER 14

THE NEXT FEW DAYS passed very slowly for Charles Muncie. The deal he had made for Chris Brown to star in a sitcom blew up when he was arrested again for assaulting his latest girlfriend. He got his Jaguar back from the shop. The repair bill was two thousand dollars. His car insurance would go up another four thousand next year. Word came back from Katherine Heigl's people that she wanted $2.5 million to meet the Global board of directors. More if she had to eat with them. A hot new Web series about talking condoms was going viral on YouTube. Charles bought it for mid–six figures but Standards and Practices had informed him the subject matter was unacceptable for going out over the air. But to compete these days you needed edgier material. The first battle was over the title. He wasn't married to *All That Jizz* and had suggested *The C-Team* instead. The fight on this project would go on for months (assuming he was still there for months).

His overall frustration level rose to the degree that he snapped at his assistant, Lana, for the first time ever. And all she did was offer to arrange for a massage.

By Saturday morning Charles was particularly surly. Sondra had arranged this fix-up disguised as a tennis date, and Charles saw no possible scenario where this ended well for him. He was also galled that Gersh would be setting foot in his house, his *sanctuary*.

Stevie arrived only an hour late. *Will he even apologize?* Charles wondered as he opened the door.

"Week and half. That's all you've got left," Stevie said, looking trim in his blinding-white tennis outfit. Charles was bulging out of his. It's hard to hide an expanding gut in shorts.

"Aren't you even going to say hello first? Or thanks for putting my show on the air? Or thanks for giving me a chance? Or sorry for keeping everyone waiting for a fucking hour?"

"Week and a half."

Typical. "Well, don't just stand there," Charles said. "Come on in. See how a fucking mercenary lives."

Stevie ignored that shot and entered the foyer. "Oh. I have to tell you, I came up with a great idea for the last episode," he said looking around, unimpressed. "In keeping with the theme that you never know what's going to happen next—we all die. The whole ensemble. It may be a problem for possible spin-offs, but I know I can do it really funny."

Charles turned to face him. "Then you'd better write it, because I'm not going to do your twisted dirty work for you." All the frustrations over the last few weeks came to a boil. "Who do you think you are? God? You are actually sick from your own success, and let me be the first person to give you the cure for it. *No!* No, Stevie. Listen to that word. *No!* I'm sure you've hardly ever heard it. Certainly not within the last five years. But *no!* No. No. No. No. No."

Stevie took the lashing in stride. "Well, I guess that's it, then. You've made your decision."

"The company is prepared to give you a private jet."

Stevie smiled and glanced over Charles' shoulder. They had reached the patio and something caught the monster's attention.

"Whoa. Hel-lo there," Stevie said catching first sight of Anji. She was leading Sondra through some stretching exercises and looked smoking in skintight workout clothes.

Charles thought, *What a lowlife scumbag.* Stevie was so distraught that the one love of his life would reject him that he ordered her killed, and yet here he was like a cartoon wolf with his eyeballs springing out of his head the minute he saw another hot piece of ass. "Her name is Anji," he said, assuming Stevie'd be in bed with her before she could count out thirty reps.

"What a body!"

"She was a runner-up in the Ms. Fitness America contest."

"Really? Who won?"

"This is all we have here *today*. Can you just picture yourself flying away to Hawaii with her in your very own Gulfstream? The G-III"

"Well, I should probably meet her," Stevie said, and he stepped through the French doors onto the patio.

Sondra spotted him first. "Look who's here! Come on over, Stevie; don't be shy."

Anji's eyes lit up. "Stevie Gersh? Shut *up!*"

Sondra introduced Anji. Stevie squinted and said, "I know you. You were in the Ms. Fitness pageant, right?"

"Yes!" Anji said, thrilled beyond belief that someone as famous as Stevie Gersh would know who she was.

Charles muttered softly, "Phony bastard." Sondra elbowed him. Hard.

On the hill above their house, from his back deck, Fox president Marc Jantzen surveyed the scene below through binoculars. He had been enjoying the early spring view—two hot women doing aerobics—when suddenly the plot thickened. Stevie Gersh was there. Marc didn't have much use for Charles as a programmer, but he did respect his tenacity. He would have to somehow address this latest turn of events.

Meanwhile, down below, out of earshot:

"So what do you do?" Stevie asked Anji.

"Trainer."

"And . . . ?" Charles said, prompting.

"And what?" said Anji.

"Don't forget *producer.*"

"Right. I'm a producer."

"Fitness-type show?" Stevie wondered.

Anji turned to Charles to help.

"Yes," he said. "I think you'd put it in the . . . fitness genre . . . of entertainment."

Click! Stevie went into his act. "Yeah, fitness, what's the story with all that fitness? I'll tell you when you're fit. After you die. Your heart rate is next to nothing. Your buns are solid as a rock. And there's so little fat on you, you don't float."

They all laughed—Charles politely, Anji hysterically. "God, you are soooo funny! Are you always this funny?"

"Yeah. If you haven't seen his HBO special," Charles mumbled under his breath. He took another sharp elbow to the ribs for his effort.

"I don't know," Stevie answered false-modestly, "I just say what pops into my head."

"God, what I wouldn't give for your head."

Stevie knew an opening, even a clumsy one, when he heard it. "Listen, after I beat Tennis the Menace here . . . ," he said, referring to the ABN president and then waiting for Anji's big laugh to die down, "would you like to get some lunch, maybe see a movie? Anything but Judd Apatow."

Anji scrunched up her face. "No, thank you. I'm seeing someone."

"You are?" said Stevie, hiding his disappointment.

"Yes. Someone I care about very, very much."

Charles was ready to strangle her. Stevie maintained his composure.

"You can't make an exception? Even for me?"

Charles silently prayed. *Dear, sweet, compassionate holy Jesus, please let Anji agree to fuck Stevie Gersh . . .*

"I really can't," she said.

. . . Or strike the bitch down with lightning and let her fry to death slowly. Amen.

A stunned Stevie just blinked. For once he didn't know what to say. Despite his rage, Charles found himself enjoying this.

"Who is this guy?" asked Sondra.

That ended the enjoyment. "Don't pry," Charles said, jumping in immediately. "You really don't want to pry."

Anji turned to Stevie. "I'm sorry, but it really wouldn't be fair to him."

Charles jumped in again. "Oh, I think—whoever he is—he'd understand. I mean, it's *Gersh.*"

"I'm really sorry."

Any qualms Charles had about putting a hit out on this trollop evaporated in smoggy air.

"Oh," Stevie said breezily. "Well . . . no worries."

Charles was surprised and impressed by how well Stevie weathered this slight. "You want to play some tennis?" he asked, deflecting the unpleasantness.

"Actually, no. What I want to do is get out of here."

Okay, there was the Stevie he knew and now had to console.

Stevie dashed back into the house as Sondra and Charles called after him.

Hmmm. What was that all about? Marc Jantzen wondered from his perch above. He hated not fully knowing a situation. Spying was helpful but incomplete. Perhaps he should have Charles' home bugged. Jantzen worked for News Corp. There had to be three hundred guys on payroll whose sole job was to set those up.

Inside the house, Stevie made a beeline for the entrance and left with a resounding door slam. Charles shook his head.

"Shit. I know him," he said to Sondra. "He's going to lock himself in his house for a week, not take any calls, and just be in a funk."

"Charles, *I'll* talk to him. It was my mistake. Let me do it."

Before he could gently tell her that was maybe the worst idea ever, she too was out the door. What else could possibly go wrong? He crossed to the cherrywood-stained bar and poured himself a hit of Maker's Mark whiskey, then downed it in one midmorning gulp. Once his eyes refocused, he glanced out the window to see Anji now jumping rope with his daughter, Kelly Rose.

"All right," he stoically said, pouring another. "Now we're in Glenn Close–ville."

****

The former Sondra Hendrickson fell in love with Charles Muncie on the first date. It was a warm spring Atlanta night and he took her to see a string quartet under the stars at Chastain Park. Then it was chocolate fondue at the Melting Pot, where Charles surprised her with a violinist. And finally, a late drink at the Mansion on Peachtree, where yet another violinist was waiting. It was easily the most romantic thing anyone had ever done for her. Years later she saw the same thing on a rerun of *Love, American Style* from the seventies, but still, Charles had to pay the musicians. They went together all through college and married shortly thereafter. Sondra always felt so lucky. She'd watch her girlfriends' relationships crash and burn time and time again. What was the appeal of outlaws, bad boys, and would-be Foo Fighters? These assholes always broke their hearts. Yes, there was danger and excitement, but ultimately these romances ended in tears, crushing disappointment, and weight gain. And yet . . . her friends always seemed so drawn to them. Truly, what was the attraction? Her man was loving and kind, and it wasn't like he was a *Boy Scout*. He was not above sitcom plagiarism.

Sondra caught up with Stevie just as he was about to gun the engine of his vintage 1962 Ferrari 250 Testarossa—or, as he liked to call it, his "Saturday car." She tapped on the passenger's side window and he invited her to climb in. She slid into the souped-up roadster and began, "Stevie, if you're going to blame anybody, blame me. I should have . . . whoa! This is awesome! What kind of car is this?"

"I have no idea," he answered.

"Well . . . it's . . . very nice."

"You were saying?"

"Right. I should have found out more about her before I tried to put you two together. That was totally stupid on my part. Sometimes I get an idea and before I can even . . . how much did this thing cost? My God!"

"I don't know that either. I'm not one of those car buyers who ask a million questions. But as for the action shiksa, don't worry. It's fine. Really. And humbling, which wasn't on my schedule today, but what the hell, huh?"

Sondra detected a sadness behind his eyes. "Lucy really hurt you, didn't she?"

Stevie remained stoic. "It's like someone came over to me, ripped my chest open, and yanked out everything inside. At least that's what I'm telling my friends."

Sondra saw right through him. "Come on. Stop that," she gently scolded.

Stevie stared off into the distance for a moment. "You know the worst part?" he said finally. "Being alone. You can't imagine what that's like."

Oh but she could.

"One day I'm waking up next to her. The next night I'm all alone. Big empty bed. Big empty room. You feel so detached from everything. So cut off. And whatever you do during the day, whatever *success* you achieve, at night you still have to come back to that same lonely place. You know there's a reason why the womb was so small. Is any of this making any goddamn sense?"

Sondra looked down at her folded hands. "What would you say if I told you I was going through the same thing?"

Stevie turned to her and their eyes met. The moment was charged. Maybe too charged. Stevie broke the ice. "Lucy left you too?"

Sondra laughed, relieved and grateful that he diffused the moment. And then he continued. "I'd say . . . I'd like to hear about it."

CHAPTER 15

IF SOMEONE ISN'T BEING screwed in Hollywood, he's being honored. Exorbitant salaries, power, and prestige aren't enough. Praise must be doled out in the form of statuettes and engraved Lucite slabs. The best kinds are the awards you *win* (although, to be more precise, the best kinds are the awards you win and Harvey Weinstein doesn't), but short of those are the charity evenings saluting you.

Most savvy charitable organizations will honor Hollywood honchos, not because they so deserve it but because they bring in the most revenue. It's the Eleanor Roosevelt rule. One year a major foundation honored arguably the finest first lady this country has ever known and they took a bath. The next year they honored some swindler movie mogul and raked it in. From then on, if you had colleagues in the industry with deep pockets and you weren't the leader of a Taliban cell, you were eligible for Man of the Year status from some philanthropic group.

Invariably, the only one in the room who doesn't realize this—even though he's been to thirty other such events and knows they're a sham—is the honoree himself. It's the same way guys fool themselves in strip clubs. A bimbo winks at one while licking the pole and immediately he assumes she "thinks he's special."

This year's B'nai B'rith Humanitarian of the Year was Charles "Praise Jesus" Muncie. The setting was the ballroom of the Century Plaza Hotel, which was large but not as large as the Beverly Hilton's International (Golden Globes) Ballroom. Industry supernovas like Barbra Streisand, David Geffen, and pretty much anyone else who resides in the Malibu Colony warrant the Beverly Hilton. Network presidents and top producers get the Century Plaza. Agents and TV personalities are feted in the Santa Monica Loews.

Still, the room was filled. Very few empty seats. Leonard Armantrout and the rest of the board "wanted" to be there, but a last-minute *crisis* required all of them to stay back in New York or fly back to New York. Among the guests who did attend were Marc Jantzen and his wife, so there was much love and warmth in the room.

Marc had just heard back from corporate that his request to bug Charles' house had been denied. Following the *News of the World* phone-hacking scandal, parent company News Corp. was backing off covert practices such as those—for the present time. The Fox president would have to find an alternate way to control the Stevie situation.

Charles and Sondra sat at the head table as Charles' mentor and former ABN president, Frank Brunner, stood at the dais bellowing the introductory speech. "Ladies and gentlemen," his resonant voice echoed, "tonight we honor a great man, Charles Muncie, this year's B'nai B'rith Humanitarian of the Year. It's quite an honor. Eleanor Roosevelt never received this. I am asked to speak at a lot of these things. Too many, really. But tonight is special for me because I consider Charles a son."

Charles' eyes scanned the room, past the enemies and bottom-feeders. A smile crossed his lips when he determined that one person in particular was not there—Anji DeVelera.

At the moment she was in nearby Brentwood, bounding out of the Pro Gym after a brisk workout. She climbed into her Camry and pulled away, turning left onto Bundy Drive and zipping right past the infamous condominium where O.J. Simpson got away with slaughtering two people.

"Oh, I'm sure everyone in this room knows Charles Muncie," Frank Brunner droned, "the young network president. But there's another side of him you might not know. The caring, generous, family-oriented man who has devoted his life to, in his words, 'the celebration of humanity.'"

Anji was famished. That StairMaster had kicked her ass. She stopped at a light on Wilshire Boulevard and couldn't help but notice a McDonald's on the corner. If she had one weakness besides sleeping with anyone she thought could further her career, it was Happy Meals. The Golden Arches beckoned. Should she or shouldn't she? She wrestled back and forth while the light remained red, but when it finally switched to green she gave in to temptation and swung into the drive-through. She deserved a break today after all the emotional angst Charles Muncie had put her through.

"In a very cynical industry, Charles has always been a positive force. When people think of television as just junk food or a guilty pleasure, he has taken steps to elevate the form."

Audience members dutifully nodded, but half were thinking, *Please let a meteor fall on this room.*

"Charles has given us shows that were thought provoking. Shows that brought us together around the water cooler. Shows that tear asunder the hypocrisy that we live with daily, and at the same time, shows that heal, that make us aware once again that we, each of us, are capable of more."

Anji, meanwhile, sat in the McDonald's parking lot unwrapping her big, juicy, sloppy, unhealthy Big Mac. She looked around. No one was watching. She'd pay for this, she thought as she sank her teeth into the fat-laden burger.

She was right.

There was a muffled sound. Anji's head lunged forward and hit the steering wheel. She slumped over, dead. A hand reached into the Camry and yanked out her purse, making it look like a robbery. It reached back in and grabbed a fry.

"And now it's my honor to introduce the man of the hour, the Man of the Year—Charles Muncie."

CHAPTER 16

THE MUNCIES LEFT THE DINNER around eleven o'clock. Charles handed his valet ticket to the non-pro and they waited at the expansive hotel entrance. Thus a few moments for reflection. The night had gone well. He was surprised by how many people congratulated him and seemed convincingly sincere. Perhaps he was overestimating the number of "enemies" he had. Maybe he was more admired in the industry than he had assumed. That was a nourishing thought . . . that lasted maybe two seconds. Was the lack of enemies due to respect or *lack* of respect?

Was he not considered dangerous enough to fear or loathe? No. There was a sense of brotherhood. And if not *true* brotherhood, then brotherhood-for-the-moment, which in Hollywood could mean the same thing.

Stevie showed up, but late. Was he still smarting from Anji's rebuff earlier that day? What had happened after he drove away? Was Stevie conflicted regarding Charles? Did tonight perhaps move him in some way? Did Judaism remind him that there was something bigger in the universe than himself? Or did he still think his tweets were more sacred than the Torah? Probably. *Look who we're dealing with.*

The car pulled up and Charles decided to table this mind debate and just concentrate on the positive aspects of this evening. Oh . . . one more mental note: What about a procedural crime series where the hook is the lead detective hears voices in his head that argue the clues amongst themselves? He then is able to sift through the din and deduce the truth. *Private Ear* or *The Chatterbrain*—something like that.

Charles generously tipped the non-pro a ten and climbed into his sporty Jaguar. Sondra slipped into the passenger side clutching his unwieldy engraved Lucite award. He eased into the light traffic on Avenue of the Stars. That street name was a joke. No stars lived there. CAA had recently relocated there. The street should be called Avenue of the Death Star.

Feeling somewhat mellow and at peace, he clicked on the radio: soft jazz on 94.7, the Wave—all Dave Koz all the time.

"I was very happy with the way that came off tonight," Sondra said.

"Yes. It was remarkable. Remarkable."

That stripper thinks I'm special.

Charles had felt so bad about himself for so long that he was entitled to savor this moment of glory, no matter how fiscally orchestrated it was. "My only regret is that my"—Charles got choked up on the next word—"mother couldn't be there to see that."

Sondra was surprised. "Charles, that's the first time you've mentioned your mother in ages."

"I don't know, I've been thinking of her a lot the last few days. I think she told me after heart attack number three, 'Don't measure success by the amount of money you make. Measure it by the amount you give away.' After tonight I feel my successes outweigh my failures."

Sondra let that big revelation hang in the air for a moment, then asked, "Does that mean we're through with TV Jesus now?"

Charles was on his own train of thought. "And the sum total," he continued, "is I'm good. And oh what a feeling that is."

A velvet voice on the radio announced that it was time for the news. "Top story this hour: a robbery/murder at a local McDonald's. Twenty-six-year-old Anji DeVelera was shot and killed in the parking lot of a Westside McDonald's this evening."

Sondra gasped. "Oh my God!"

Charles said nothing. A chill shimmered through his body. He was frozen.

"Ms. DeVelera was the third-place finisher in this year's Ms. Fitness America pageant. The murder is under investigation. Police at this hour have no suspects."

Sondra was beside herself. "We saw her just today. Oh my God!" Charles stared ahead at the road. He was numb, in shock, stupefied.

That expression would not change all night as he sat alone in his office in the dark. The magnitude of what he had done absolutely paralyzed him. Hiring hit men, killing folks—those things only happened to other people. People like Charles Muncie, good, God-fearing people—they only green-lit pilots *about* incidents like that.

This was like Woody Allen's *Crimes and Misdemeanors*, he noted in his mishmash of thoughts. And Woody Allen's *Match Point*, which was essentially the same movie. How can a reputable man, who believes in family and ethics and gun control, live with the guilt and shame of committing such an unspeakable act? God, Martin Landau was good in *Crimes and Misdemeanors*. Focus. There was also the issue of hiding the guilt. Was Charles capable of that? That Zen shit wasn't going to cut it here. This required legitimate *acting*. Was he a good enough actor? Oh, he took an acting class in high school, but primarily that was because he had heard there were a lot of cute girls and very few guys, and he did get to do that rape scene from *Elmer Gantry* with Karen Siegel, but nothing ever came of it. Whatever happened to Karen Siegel? She had great eyes. But a squeaky voice now that Charles thought about it. Really squeaky. Downright annoying after a while. Was she married? Did that voice drive her husband crazy? Was he convincing in the scene? Did Woody Allen win Best Screenplay for *Crimes and Misdemeanors*? Do hit men use one gun or do they discard the murder weapon after every kill and get a new one so they ultimately can't be charged with multiple homicides? Do the ends really justify the means? *Justified*—damn, that was another great show he wished ABN had. What was Karen like in bed? She was always very sensuous. Imagine those beautiful brown eyes looking up at you. What did she sound like in bed? At the height of passion did garage doors go up all over the neighborhood when she screamed? But he bet that her husband, no matter how aggravated, never hired an assassin to kill her at McDonald's. Holy shit! What had he done? Landau got an Oscar nomination for *Crimes and Misdemeanors*—that he knew.

This went on for hours. Stray thoughts overlapping one another, mental white noise in search of clarity. Among the fragments: looking for religious loopholes, flimsy rationalizations, a list of actors he felt were good enough to pull this charade off, would there be an investigation, a comparison of *Crimes and Misdemeanors* and *Match Point*—especially the endings (he liked *Crimes* way better because Landau decides at some point to just say "fuck it" and move on), if there's an investigation, speculation over whether it would lead to him, an idea for a show where normal people try to get away with murder (but how would they test with focus groups?), and could he lay off that idea with the hit man whom he realized he still owed a series commitment.

The first light of day streaked through the window. Charles blinked for the first time in four hours. His cell phone buzzed. The overnights had arrived. Survival instincts took over and he snapped out of his haze. He shook his head, ran his hands through his quickly graying hair, and snatched the phone. The *Gersh* rerun was the most watched show of the night.

CHAPTER 17

CHARLES DRESSED QUICKLY and was out of the house while Sondra and Kelly Rose were still asleep. Facing them would have been just too excruciating. And if women can sense poontang on their men, surely they can sense blood. The best course of action would be to throw himself into his work. It was only after he got out of his car that he noticed he was wearing brown shoes with a blue suit.

At his desk, in the comfort of his palatial office, where it was at least *presumed* he was a man worthy of such lofty trappings, Charles began to unclench for the first time since hearing the shocking news. He allowed himself to finally entertain the upside of this tragedy. Yes, there was one. Anji was out of his life for good. No more would she stalk him, no more would she threaten the sanctity and stability of his treasured marriage. Now no one would ever know about the affair. *Dead dingbats tell no tales.*

No, he wasn't letting himself off the hook, but he was reaching deep down for that positive attitude that had served him so well. As the old expression sort of goes, "Hand someone Lemon Springs Rat Poisoning and they'll make lemonade."

Sticking to the plan, he focused on his work. He had Tara Durban coming in at two o'clock. For months he had courted her to do a series for ABN. So he figured he better watch some episodes of *Bitches*. He had seen the pilot and hadn't responded to it, but that was before it exploded into a huge hit on HBO. At only twenty-two years old, Tara Durban was now being touted as the voice of her generation. He watched several episodes, and try as he might, he couldn't find anything remotely funny. *This won the Golden Globe for Best* Comedy? he kept saying to himself. Usually whenever there was a disconnect between his tastes and the country's he just assumed he was the one in the wrong. And he was usually right. But in this case he was pretty sure, despite the accolades bestowed on the show by the two dozen or so waiters who call themselves the Hollywood Foreign Press, that *Bitches* was bleak and cynical and gratuitously vulgar. Still, Charles was desperate to have Tara Durban do one just like it for him.

As he scanned the Net for positive reviews of *Bitches* so he'd have something complimentary and informed to say, his assistant, Lana, buzzed him. "Charles, your two o'clock is here."

"Marvelous! Send Ms. Durban in."

He junked the remainder of the Caesar salad he was eating at his desk and straightened his tie.

Lana continued: "Oh . . . and there are also two detectives from the LAPD who want to talk to you."

"Detectives?"

"Yes. They showed me their badges. These are not just actors sneaking past security."

"Did they say what they want?"

"No. They just want to speak with you."

"All right. Send them in."

"That means you're going to keep Tara Durban waiting."

"Just send them in!"

Shit! How did they find him? And so *soon*? TV detectives would take two days, follow three false leads, and have to chase a weasel through two alleys and up a fire escape to zero in on the real suspect. Charles took a deep breath, silently prayed to Jesus or "whoever actually *is* the Supreme Being," and stood to welcome his guests.

Lana ushered in Detective Staley and Detective Long. Both were in their thirties but looked like they were in their forties. They wore suits obviously purchased on sale at J.C. Penney or Ross Dress for Less. Both outfits required alterations and dry cleaning. But at least they matched the shoes.

Charles came out from behind his desk to greet them.

"Gentlemen, welcome to ABN," he said, shaking their hands. "How can I assist you?"

"Mr. Muncie, I'm Detective Daniel Staley and this is Detective Robbie Long. We're from the LAPD Homicide Division investigating a murder/robbery that occurred last night. Anji DeVelera."

Lana returned to her office to babysit the wunderkind.

Charles invited the detectives to sit on his overstuffed couch while he pulled up a chair across from them.

"Yes. Anji. I heard last night driving home from a charity event." He made sure to slip in his alibi right up front. "It's a tragedy of the spirit, a tragedy of the times. We mourn her and we celebrate her."

Detective Long cut through the double-talk. "So you knew Ms. DeVelera?"

"Yes, yes," Charles confirmed. "I employed her as a masseuse. She also trained my wife. She finished third in the Ms. Fitness America contest, you know."

"We know very well. Actually, we have a picture of her up in our office," said Detective Long. "Kind of like an unofficial mascot. It's one of the reasons why we really want to solve this."

The pit in Charles stomach grew to the size of a coconut. "Well . . . I think we all want that," he said.

Detective Staley chimed in. "Mr. Muncie, in going through her apartment today we discovered a diary that she had kept. Did you know about said diary?"

A *diary*?! Shit!

"N-n-no," he replied, feeling the blood drain from his body.

"A rather intimate one. Were you aware that she was in love with you?"

Even from the grave that gold digger was going to torture him. Charles took a moment, steadied himself, and tried desperately to maintain his signature composure. "Well, I do hold a certain position and status. I was the B'nai B'rith Humanitarian of the Year."

"I don't think that's why she liked you, sir," said Detective Long.

His partner continued, "She speaks about an afternoon she spent with you at the San Bernardino Courtyard by Marriott in very vivid detail."

"Dear God!"

"She was quite a good writer. Very Danielle Steele–esque, wouldn't you say, Robbie?"

"Not as repetitive as Danielle, but yeah, certainly in that ballpark."

"Who else knows about this diary?"

"No one else, sir. And to answer your next question, we plan on keeping it on the QT."

"Yes, it would certainly compromise your investigation if something like that did get out."

"Your sorry ass is safe."

Charles nodded gratefully. "Well, I don't know what else is in that diary, but I will admit to you, not officially, that we did have a onetime tryst."

His intercom buzzed.

"Excuse me, gentlemen," Charles said as he pushed the talk-back button.

"Charles, Tara Durban is getting real mad out here."

"Fuck her! I'm busy!" Charles snapped, then returned to the detectives, all smiles. "Anyway, it was my understanding that it was over. You'll notice it was only that one time. And I'm sure there were others."

"Oh yes. According to the book there were at least fifty suitors."

"Fifty?"

"Yes, sir. It reads like the Who's Who of the Producers Guild."

"But you're the only one she professed to love."

He still needed a second to process *fifty*.

"With all due respect, gentlemen, she was confusing her love for me with her love for Jesus."

"Whoa! Someone thinks a little highly of himself."

"What? No, no. I meant our *shared* love for Jesus." Charles was trying to keep it together, but the seams were beginning to show. He steered the conversation back to the breakup.

"I happened to have the opportunity to introduce her to my wife, which was odd, but in a way a confirmation of my closure with her in matters uh . . . bodily."

"And would you know of anyone who might have wanted to harm her?" Detective Staley asked, taking out an iPad mini to use as a notepad.

"I don't know. She was in such a cutthroat competitive field. Any one of the other fitness finalists could be another Tonya Harding. Who finished *fourth*? And for my money, anyone at CAA could be a suspect for anything. I'd question them about Kennedy. And didn't you say you thought it was a robbery?"

"Correct, but we're checking all leads," said Detective Staley.

"We *really* want to solve this," said Detective Long.

"No more so than I," Charles answered reassuringly. "I regret what happened, but I don't regret having met her and known her."

"I can understand that. You two had quite a day at the ol' Marriott. Nothing about your shared religious beliefs, but she spoke glowingly of your cunnilingus technique. Really appreciated how pleasing her was important to you."

"Yes, well, I've always believed that desire comes from *being* desired."

Staley had the iPad mini at the ready. He didn't write that down.

"Didn't Michael Douglas get cancer from that?"

"That's never been proven."

"Still, it gives you pause."

His partner chimed in. "Well, assuming it is safe, just how do you perfect a technique for going down on a woman? I know they say you need ten thousand hours of practice before you really get good at something, but I sure don't want to spend ten thousand hours down there, if you know what I mean."

"Oh, I do," agreed Staley. "But really, Mr. Muncie. What's your secret?"

"Gentlemen, I'm late for a very important meeting," Charles said, losing patience and hiding embarrassment.

"Oh right," Detective Staley said, rising. "That's the young lady from *Bitches* out there, is it not?"

"Indeed."

"So what is the appeal of that show? Seriously. All those girls are spoiled little sluts. There's not one of 'em that I can root for. Can you root for any of 'em, Robbie?"

"The stuck-up little redhead, yeah. But that's because she's hot more than anything else. Her I'd give a little *lip service*, if you know what I mean."

"Oh, 'deed I do."

Charles interrupted, "If there's nothing else, gentlemen, I say we adjourn on that happy note. Thank you for your discretion. And if there's any way I can be of further assistance, please don't hesitate to call. Actually, *calling* would be preferable."

Staley and Long stood and shook hands with Charles.

"We'll keep you posted," Detective Long assured him.

Thank God they were finally leaving. Charles was practically jumping out of his skin. The two plainclothesmen crossed to the door, but just before they were about to exit, Staley turned back.

"Oh. There is one thing."

"Yes?" Charles said apprehensively.

"You know, my partner and I got to gabbing over coffee and we've got an idea for a show. You probably thought that was a '*Columbo* moment' just now, didn't ya? You know. He's just going to ask you one more thing and then drops the bomb on you."

They both laughed. Charles joined in politely. He didn't know whether to feel relief or rage.

Staley pressed on. "Now, the one thing we haven't seen on television is *real* detectives solving *real* cases. If you put a camera in a car and followed two homicide detectives around . . . We've seen patrol officers settling domestic disputes . . . Bo-ring! I'm talking hard-core crime. Murder. Manslaughter. Arson. Gang wars are a stretch for us, but hey, there's creative license. '*Staley and Long*—Tuesday at ten.' It could work, sir."

"Well, we're not really in the market for a reality-based police show at the moment," Charles said, hustling them out the door.

Both detectives were disappointed but covered by saying, "No problem," "Totally understand," "It was just a thought." Then Long said, "One more thing. So how come you didn't return her phone calls?"

"Let me sleep on your idea," Charles said immediately. "There may be some merit to it."

"That's all we ask."

"You have a good day, sir."

They left the room finally and Charles closed the door and almost collapsed. He staggered back to his desk and buried his head in his hands.

The intercom buzzed, snapping him out of it. He scrambled for his notes. *Bitches* was a bold first step in transforming television from a mindless carrier of unrealistic dreams into a reflection of society as it really exists. And only with our eyes wide open could we as a people grow and evolve. *Bitches* wasn't just a comedy (if it was even that)—it was *important*. But now it was time for Tara Durban to take the next big step—the career choice that would define her as either a mere flavor of the month or a true genius. Could she do it again but without nudity? That was the gauntlet Charles Muncie was prepared to lay at her feet, along with a firm series commitment and ballplayer money.

"Send Ms. Durban in. I'm ready," Charles said over the intercom.

Tara Durban, dressed for a business meeting with a network president in torn blue jeans and a ratty T-shirt, stormed into the office. Charles never got the chance to deliver his pitch. For ten minutes she *motherfucked* him up and down. He made her wait; he was rude; he was an asshole—one F-bomb after another. Never in his career had anyone ripped into him like this. She was relentless, vicious, and with utter disregard for his position and stature in the industry. And when she finally ran out of steam and the last *you fucking cunt* had been uttered, she was shocked when he threw his arms around her and said, "Thanks for sending your messenger, Jesus. I hear you, O Lord."

CHAPTER 18

SONDRA GAZED OUT AT the Pacific Ocean. Not many beach-goers this weekday in mid-March despite the appearance of a pleasant day. In any other part of the country it would be termed *unseasonably warm*, but in Southern California it was just Thursday. And residents of the Malibu Colony spent more time keeping people *off* their beaches than using them themselves.

Sondra stood on the balcony and propped her elbows on the wood railing. The breeze flowed through her matted hair. What was she doing there, clad only in a fluffy white robe with the *Gersh* logo on the breast pocket? Not that she didn't feel sublime. That was some really hot sex. She finally understood the attraction of bad boys. Sondra was sure she'd feel less sublime driving back into town in a couple of hours to pick Kelly Rose up from school, but for now she savored the afterglow. Unlike her husband, she was capable of doing that. She could allow herself a moment's peace.

Besides, this was all her husband's fault. Charles drove her to this. How many months had he shut her out? How many warnings had she sounded? He had drifted so far from her that he was like that speck of an oil barge way out on the distant horizon.

And then last night.

After hearing the horrible news of Anji DeVelera's death, Charles clammed up completely. It was eerie, almost chilling. For the rest of the night. Not a word. She tried to talk to him, commiserate, even just squeeze his hand, but he just closed himself off, an impenetrable shell. He went into his home office and never even turned on the light. Who was this man? This . . . zombie? This . . . bat?

For months she had blamed the job. That was what had created this wedge between them. But now she realized it was something else, something deeper. If he couldn't talk to her—and she wasn't insisting he share his innermost secrets and fears, although she *was* his life partner—if he couldn't say friggin' *hello*, there was something seriously wrong.

Stevie Gersh had been so sweet to her yesterday in his car. She saw a vulnerable side she didn't know existed. And just the fact that a man would open himself up to her was in itself a refreshing change. And surprisingly stimulating.

By the time she awoke this morning, Charles had already left. No kiss on the forehead, no little note on the fridge, no text message. It was as if he were actively avoiding her. Why? What about this fitness trainer's death so traumatized him?

And then it hit her. Of course! Duh! He had to be sleeping with her. And more than that, he had to really *care* about her. Otherwise, why would he be so distraught? It wasn't like she was starring in one of his network's successful shows. That son of a bitch was having an affair. Now she was furious, hurt, and humiliated. And she had to let it out. The teakettle was about to blow. She had to spill her feelings to someone, *anyone*. How convenient that Stevie Gersh happened to call and ask how she was faring after the tragic news. And when she told him how stressed she was, how considerate to offer her a ride in his spiffy *Saturday* Ferrari.

Wasn't her cheating on Charles the same as his cheating on her? No, she had rationalized. There was a difference. Charles' affair was emotional. Hers was just two wounded jilted souls seeking temporary relief from their heartbreak. Three times in one hour! Sondra would have to give Stevie some tips on performing oral sex like she did with Charles, but overall this was just what she needed. And the distinction was clear, at least to her. What Charles had was a *love affair*; this was a *hookup*.

Stevie joined her on his balcony, also wearing nothing but a robe. He draped his arm around her and she nestled into his neck.

"It's so beautiful out here," she cooed.

"Yes. Thank God for those sandbags."

****

"I want thirteen on the air and I want total creative control." Tara Durban said emphatically. "And by that I mean no network interference of any kind. No script notes. No casting approval. No final edit. I don't run story areas by you. I don't turn in outlines. I choose my staff. There's none of those gross little animated promos you run at the bottom of the screen. 'Hi, I'm some idiot from an ABN sitcom. Look how zany I am because I'm waving my arms distracting you and totally taking you out of the show you're currently watching. But who gives a shit because *my* show is on tomorrow night at nine.' Ugh! Ugh and obscene."

Charles just nodded, not listening to a single word she said.

"End credits have to be full screen. You can't shrink them into the corner so you can promote some new reality-slash-dating-slash-singing show hosted by Ryan Seacrest. I have approval over the commercials. The fastest way to go from cool to really uncool is to show Flo from Progressive Insurance.

"The censors have to give me some room. I understand the realities. You have the FCC, and one Bible-thumping old crone in Arkansas sends a letter and everyone freaks as if you were showing penetration, but it's not the 1990s anymore. We don't say *master of his domain*; we say *masturbate*. It's an actual word in the dictionary, as are *anal* and *creampie*. So I'll give you a choice, because again, I'm not unreasonable—either let me say it or show it.

"Oh, and one other thing. I insist we do the show live. I want America to say, 'Oh fuck! Did they really just do that?' Those are the parameters, and once you've agreed to all of them I can start thinking about what the show should be. I don't have any thoughts at the moment, but I'm thinking incest is a theme we haven't seen in family sitcoms, so . . ."

Charles put his hand up. "Tara, could you hold that thought for one moment?"

"Why?" she said, aghast that anyone would dare interrupt her.

"I'll be right back."

Charles patted her on the shoulder, then briskly stepped out of the office. As he passed Lana on his way out the double doors, he said, "I'm not feeling well. I'm going home."

"What about Tara?" Lana called out after him.

But he was gone.

Charles climbed into his Jag and started for home. The minute he was past the guard gate, he began to cry. Uncontrollably. His life was ruined. He was a total failure . . . at everything. How proud would his mother be now? The B'nai B'rith Humanitarian of the Year. What a joke! Come to think of it, she wasn't even that fond of Jews.

Zipping down Sunset past San Vicente and the old Whiskey a Go Go of the legendary Strip days, an idea occurred to him. The tears began to subside and his composure slowly returned. He could feel himself coming out of his despair. He continued driving, passing the demarcation where the office buildings and nightclubs of West Hollywood ended and the famous palm-tree-lined streets of Beverly Hills began. This once signified Hollywood royalty. Now it signified Iranian royalty. The wheels turned in Charles' head. For the first time in a day a slight smile crossed his lips. A change of plans. He would take Sunset Boulevard all the way down to the beach.

CHAPTER 19

THERE ARE ONLY TWO SPEEDS when you drive Pacific Coast Highway—eighty and three. You either fly or there are mudslides and beach traffic. This was an eighty day. In no time Charles pulled up in front of Stevie Gersh's Malibu Colony home. He bounded out of the car, crossed to the heavy front door, and feverishly rang the bell. There was no answer. He rang it again. Finally, Stevie's muffled and annoyed voice came over the squawk box.

"Who is it?"

"Charles Muncie."

There was a lonnnnnng moment of silence.

"It's a bad time."

Charles stabbed the talk-back button. "Damn, it, I drove all the way out here!"

"Who asked you to?"

"Open the door!"

"Sorry, Chuck. It's got to be another time."

Charles was livid. "Stevie, your wanton impertinence for me aside—"

"What?"

"Disrespect. Your disrespect aside—"

"No. Wanton. What does that mean?"

"Um . . . excessive, I think. The point is I must speak to you. And I am not leaving until you open this fucking door and let me in!"

He began pounding on that fucking door. "Stevie, I sandbagged this house. I saved it!"

The door finally opened a crack and Stevie appeared, still dressed as before. "All right, what do you want?" he snarled.

"Oh. You're with someone," Charles said noticing the robe. "That's good. That's a very heartening sign. Who is she?"

"What do you want?"

"I'm not going to stand out here. Let me come in for a moment. I want to propose something and I don't want to do it outside."

"The place is such a mess."

"Oh, for crissakes!" Charles said and pushed past his host into the house. Stevie subtly blocked him in the foyer, preventing him from entering the high-ceilinged, almost-glass-enclosed living room. From the living room TV *Ellen* could be heard.

"All right. Quick," said Stevie.

Charles was too excited to wait any longer. "Okay, how can I put this? Lucy's not the one you really want dead. The one who really rejected you—humiliated you even—was Anji, the little fitness girl. Now . . . as a show of good faith . . . we at ABN have eradicated Anji."

Stevie blinked. He wasn't sure he'd heard right.

"What?!"

"Killed."

"No, I got that. Are you fucking kidding?"

"Just hear me out. I will admit this latest turn of events was not in the original game plan, but as it says in the Holy Bible, 'Whatever has come to be has already been named, and it is known what man is, and that he is not able to dispute with one stronger than he.' And as such we think we have satisfied your condition."

"You're serious?"

"You're damned right I'm serious. We live in both a spiritual garden and an entertainment jungle."

Even Stevie was at a loss for words. "I . . . I don't believe this," he managed to say.

"I'm trying to get my next season set. I've got issues at home to deal with. I'm not exactly the perfect husband and father. Tell me it's done, Stevie. For godsakes, you've put me through hell already."

Stevie waved his arms in disbelief. "I don't want Anji dead. Are you fucking nuts? She means nothing to me. I don't want anybody dead!"

"What?"

"I'm in a better place now."

Now it was Charles who couldn't believe what he was hearing. "Nobody?"

"God, no. Live and let live."

"So that's it?"

"That's it."

"A better place? You're in a *better place*? Everything's now fine? Everything's just hunky-dory? Live and let live. The sky is blue; the grass is green. Children are playing. Everyone is singing 'Kumbaya.'"

"Yeah."

"Oh God. You sick bastard!"

"Well . . . come on."

"You're the devil!"

"Excuse me, but I've worked hard for that leverage."

Charles started to swoon. "Oh no. My chest . . . I can't breathe . . . I can't breathe," he gasped.

Charles slipped past Stevie and crossed, wobbling, through the living room.

"Air . . . I need air."

"Wait! No. Charles. Wait!"

On the flat screen, Ellen was getting relationship advice from Teri Hatcher.

Weaving through the room, Charles slid open the large glass patio doors and staggered out onto the balcony, unaware that Sondra was sitting on a lounge chair.

She froze, panicked. Charles leaned over the redwood railing and began hyperventilating.

Suddenly it hit him and he whirled around to see his wife in her matching *Gersh* bathrobe.

"Sondra?!"

Stevie joined them on the balcony.

"You know, this would make a great episode," he said trying to break the tension.

"Oh my God! Oh my *fucking God*!" screamed Charles.

Sondra sprang to her feet and tried desperately to placate him. "Charles, please . . ."

The robe came open. This did not aid her cause.

He was beside himself. All those voices in his head were chattering at once. "No! No!" he said, windmilling his arms. "I just want to get out of here!"

He rushed inside with Sondra calling after him and retying her robe.

Stevie and Sondra followed Charles into the living room and tried to catch him as he scrambled to the front door. A news report from the television, however, stopped everyone in their tracks.

"There's a new development today in the death of fitness queen Anji DeVelera. A KABN investigation unit, working in conjunction with *TMZ*, has learned of a secret diary removed from the victim's apartment. In it, among other things, is a detailed description of a torrid affair between Ms. DeVelera and ABN president Charles Muncie."

"Oh Jesus!"

"What?!"

"At the moment, our own Mr. Muncie is not a suspect. But he does have some explaining to do. Our team coverage now begins as we go first, live, to the Courtyard by Marriott in San Bernardino."

"You son of a bitch!" Sondra screamed.

"Me? What about you?!" Charles screamed back.

"You brought her into my house!"

"Actually, *you* did."

"You fucked her!"

"You fucked *him*!"

"You fucked her first!"

"But you didn't *know* I fucked her first. So until this moment, technically, you fucked him first."

"That's ridiculous!"

"No, it's not. Intent is nine-tenths of the law."

"That's *possession* is nine-tenths of the law."

"Intent is a form of possession."

"You drove me to this! And what you just said was stupid!"

"You wanted separate bedrooms!"

"You drove me to that, too."

"Well, you sure managed to drive yourself *here*," Charles retorted. "Of all the people, Sondra. Of all the people! You fucked *him*! If Hitler was funny, that's who you let enter you!"

"Hey, here," Stevie chimed in, "I'm going to say it right now, here, to both of you, so you hear it from my mouth. I'm going to do three more seasons! That's right. Not one, not two, but three! Huh? Champagne?"

That did little to assuage Charles. His parting words were from the Bible. "As for the cowardly, the faithless, the detestable, the sexually immoral, sorcerers, idolaters, and all liars, their portion will be in the lake that burns with fire and sulfur, which is the second death!"

And with that he stomped out, slamming the large redwood door so hard, every floor-to-ceiling window in the house rattled worse than they had during the last three earthquakes.

Charles started for the car, then turned back. He unzipped his fly and pissed on Stevie's front door. A passing Beemer honked in support. With his free hand, Charles acknowledged with the Black Power fist salute.

Satisfied with his defiant albeit feeble gesture, he triumphantly zipped up, hopped in his Jaguar, gunned the engine for show, and roared away.

But to where?

CHAPTER 20

HOME WAS THE LAST PLACE he wanted to go. No, the *office* was the last—home was second to last. He was a man without a sanctuary

Other alternatives: A church? Screw that! If this was how Jesus watched over His flock, He was more incompetent than the idiot Bryn Mawr grad Charles hired to oversee current programming.

Drowning his sorrows in a nice seaside bar was his next thought. All that nautical shit and Oysterettes instead of mixed nuts. He loved Oysterettes. Yes, they were just soda crackers, but they were bite-sized and had a slightly thicker consistency. Also, anyone who'd be in a dark bar at the beach had to be at least as miserable as he was.

But invariably the bartender or waitress or sad sack sitting on the next stool was an actor he had once rejected. All he wanted was a lousy beer, but the barkeep would say, "I got a master's degree from Emerson, was in Second City Chicago for two years, replaced Jeff Foxworthy in the tour of *The Producers*, and yet you pass on me for Carson Daly? He couldn't be funny if he was wearing *two* chicken suits!" Then Charles would be charged twenty dollars for a Miller Lite.

He didn't need any of those all-too-familiar confrontations. Besides, those bars always had TVs going. He didn't need to be reminded of his indiscretion with *exclusive new details* emerging on how he used a phony name from *Mission Impossible*.

He needed someplace open where he could be alone to think. Hey, how about the beach? It was quiet, secluded—and also in its favor, he was already *there*.

Charles revved the high-performance engine and sped to Zuma. Farther up the coast from the "Bu," Zuma was the locals' beach of choice. Very few tourists ventured that far north, the waves were too small for surfers, so all that was left was San Fernando Valley residents with faulty or no air-conditioning. But they invaded only on the weekends. Charles parked in a practically deserted lot, removed his brown shoes, rolled up his Armani suit pants, and padded his way through the cool sand to the shore.

Wooly dark clouds were beginning to drift in from the west. The setting sun was obscured, so there would be no majestic sunset this night. A breeze kicked in. In the Midwest these would be warning signs of an impending storm. Here it meant "get your sweater from the car."

Charles stood alone on the vast white beach. For several moments he could just suspend time. All of his many crushing messy crises would have to be dealt with, but none at this very second. He could wiggle his toes in the powdery sand, free of any human interaction. There was no one in sight in any direction. He closed his eyes and helped himself to a couple of deep, healthy breaths. The salty air tasted good, comforting, revitalizing. Yes, if ever there was the definition of *oasis . . .*

Then his cell phone chirped.

Charles checked the caller ID. *Oh hell!*

"Hello?"

"Charles, it's Leonard." CEO Leonard Armantrout and several of the board members were dining at Le Bernadin in Manhattan with Katherine Heigl. "Well. You've certainly got your tits in a ringer, haven't you?"

Charles thought, as with most oases, this one disappeared with a poof. Oh wait. Those were mirages.

"Good news, sir," Charles said, switching to autopilot. "Gersh has agreed to three more years."

"Old news!" Armantrout barked. "He told us this morning."

"Pardon me?"

"He's in love, reenergized—bullshit, bullshit, bullshit. Whoever this broad is, she must be one incredible lay."

Charles' ass was so clenched it could have crushed coal into diamonds.

"But the point is, Charles, he's in the fold. You, on the other hand, have become an embarrassment to this very high-profile conglomerate. I heard the news story. Don't deny it. This wasn't a CNN report, so it had to be true."

"There were extenuating circumstances that in a very roundabout way were beneficial to the network. To the layman it's a diary, but to the truly informed it's really a development report."

Armantrout cut him off. "We can't have this smarmy blemish on our organization, an organization built on family values."

One of the board members brushed his leg against Katherine Heigl's, causing her to slap it away.

"So how can I say this . . . ?" he continued.

Charles had had it. He knew what was coming. He was tired of fighting. Tired of spinning.

"I'm fired? Are those the words you're so delicately trying to convey? I'm axed? I'm blown out? Canned? Sacked? Kicked to the curb? Getting my walking papers? Given my pink slip? Eighty-sixed? Fucked in the ass? Stop me when one of these phrases best approximates your corporate intention."

"We have serious concerns about your judgment. I mean, seriously, the Courtyard by Marriott San Bernardino?"

"So what do *you* use? The Red Roof Inn Paramus?"

"Terminated. That is the official word for what you now are. Terminated with official prejudice and unofficial delight."

"Contact my attorney and work out my nice, big fat settlement, you prick. Thanks to you, I'll be having my next affair at the Four Seasons on Maui."

"You're being dismissed on a morals clause. That nice big fat settlement is pulled off the table. So it's back to Berdoo, I'm afraid."

"What? You can't do that!"

"See you in court . . . in ten years."

"You motherfucker! You want to play hardball? You think you can push me around? Fine. I'll beat you in court. And I'll beat your network. I'll go elsewhere and hand you your fucking head!"

Armantrout laughed. "Are you kidding? After this? After you've become the laughingstock of the industry? After you've disrespected a major conglomerate? Who do you think owns the other networks? *Other* major conglomerates. And guess what? We all *talk*!"

"That's collusion."

"See you in *that* court in ten years. You're through, Muncie. Out of the business. For good. Forever. You still want to work in television? I hear Al-Manar is looking for a head of children's programming."

"Just call my fucking lawyer!"

"I will . . . although I imagine he's already quite busy."

"Fuck you! Fuck you! Fuck! You!"

CHAPTER 21

CHARLES HUNG UP THE PHONE and hurled it forty feet into the ocean. For several moments he just stood there, shaking.

The waves lapped up on the shore, almost beckoning him. He moved towards them. The white suds of a breaker at its last gasp advanced on Charles and splashed over his feet. A shiver went up his spine. Damn, that water was cold! A few more waves and his feet adjusted. Now the water just felt cool, refreshing. He moved in a few more steps. The cold water engulfed his ankles.

He was ruined. He'd *thought* he was ruined before, but like in everything else, he was wrong. *Now* he was really, officially, irrevocably ruined. His marriage was in shambles. His daughter would never love him again—not in the same way. She was too young to understand. For now she would be siding with Mommy. And Mommy, meanwhile, was blowing *der Führer*. His career was kaput. Armantrout was right. Any respect he had accumulated in the industry was gone. There would be no *elder statesman* status for him. No visiting professorship at Yale. Or even Cal State Lutheran, Thousand Oaks. Just snickering. Bad jokes on Letterman. Worse jokes on Ferguson. Constant humiliation. To quote the famous Hollywood phrase: "He can never have lunch in this town again."

He kept walking. The water was at knee level, past his rolled-up pant legs. Jesus Christ, it was frigid! Why the hell do people ever go in the ocean out here? The temperature had to be sixty degrees. The Atlantic was warm. This was nuts.

Not that he could see behind the granite clouds, but the sun was now slowly setting. No longer could Charles just ride off into his own personal sunset. With no golden parachute, all he had left was the equity in his house, car, investments, and savings. And Sondra would get half of that. If he drew from his pension, he would have to pay huge penalty fines, not to mention taxes. He did a quick calculation in his head and determined that with legal fees, the divorce, child support, capital gains, taxes, accounting, and the general state of the economy, he could be bankrupt in four to six years.

The surf began to crash against him. He was now elbow high. His soaked Armani suit felt like an anchor. He continued to trudge forward, step by laborious step.

He envisioned a brutish future of living in a cheesy one-bedroom apartment in Canoga Park, taking two months to assemble one Ikea dresser and the drawers still never slid right. His place would be *The Honeymooners* apartment. One dresser, a tiny kitchenette pushed against a wall, and a wooden table with his Lucite B'nai B'rith Humanitarian of the Year trophy sitting on it . . . unless they demanded it back.

A wave almost knocked him over, but Charles remained erect. He spit out a mouthful of saltwater. His eyes were stinging.

He was too young for a pension but way too old to start a new career. And what career? Setting aside his tarnished reputation, what else was Charles Muncie qualified to do? What pharmaceutical firm, for example, valued scheduling comedy blocks and reality nights? And his chief asset, his ability to remain cool under pressure—he just pissed on an associate's house in full view of passing traffic and then shouted obscenities to a Wall Street giant. *Don't expect to be recruited for* The Hurt Locker.

And the indignities continued. Another wave crashed over him, leaving a long strand of seaweed dangling from his ear.

What woman would have him now? Pushing middle age, suddenly renowned for philandering, with enough financial and emotional baggage to fill a cargo bin—Quasimodo would get more hits on Match.com. *That was* who Charles was walking like, dragged down by his saturated suit—Quasimodo. He was trying to think of the name (among everything else).

But the women—no longer did Charles have that *power* thing working for him. No longer could he help an impressionable young actress like Anji DeVelera.

Oh yes, Anji. He had committed first-degree murder. Or maybe second. There was also *that*. He had to deal with the constant suffocating guilt and those two dogged gumshoes—they were clearly on a personal mission. Maybe they would somehow be able to connect Charles to Robert, the hit man. He didn't know how, but he'd seen enough cop shows to know it was possible. Sooner or later Charles might be escorted past his Canoga Park neighbors in cuffs—one of those neighbors being his former gardener.

How much disgrace could one proud man handle? The icy water was up to his shoulders, now his neck. The undertow was pulling at his legs like tentacles. His eyes were burning. His ears were ringing. His legs felt like lead.

One more step and it would all be over. All the pain, all the complications, poof—like the oasis, er . . . mirage. The laughter would be replaced by sympathy. Surely he'd warrant a segment on *Entertainment Tonight*. Maybe even before the premiere party for *G.I. Joe 4*.

And the best part was—his death would be perceived as an accident. He was just out taking a swim. Wait a minute. He was still wearing his suit. Who goes for a swim in the ocean in a suit? He'd look foolish again. Even in death he'd be a joke.

A wave came along, and *whoosh*! He was swept off his feet. Charles was in a whirlpool, underwater. He frantically waved his arms, flipped over, and popped back up. He gasped for air. The next wave was maybe a moment away. This pounding would repeat. How many times could he withstand it? One of these times he would be overpowered. He would become disoriented under the water. The world would spin and there would be no relief, no popping up. He would be swept out to sea, hurtled into the black abyss.

What would his funeral be like? The last thoughts of a drowning man. Everyone in the industry would be there. Well, most of them at least. How many who wouldn't spend a thousand dollars to see him honored would pay a thousand dollars to see this?

Another wave, another dunking, once through the rinse cycle, then another reprieve.

Oh shit! Stevie Gersh would probably give the eulogy.

No! He couldn't let that happen!

This suicide was a terrible idea. What was he thinking? This was not the time to get real down on himself, but he had to acknowledge that for someone so savvy, his judgment just in general really sucked of late.

"When Charles told me he was meeting the Little Mermaid about maybe doing a series for ABN, I told him, 'Let her come to *you*.'" Stevie would get big laughs. "Seeing Charles in that coffin, I can't help thinking—does anybody still sell waterbeds?"

Charles called out, "I have to live! I have to . . . gloppp!"

The next punishing wave tossed him around like a rag doll, but damn it, he emerged.

"I have to breathe!" he now called out.

And then, in the distance, another voice was heard. Faintly.

"Charles! Charles! Charles!"

Was this another oa— . . . mirage? He turned his head to the sound.

There on the shore, waving her arms wildly, was Lucy Adamson. She wore a sheer white flowing sundress and was framed in a shaft of setting sunlight that pierced through the ominous clouds, creating an almost celestial aura.

She waded out into the frigid brine.

Slam! Another wave upended him. "Stop that already!" he shouted to the Pacific Ocean when he finally reappeared.

With strong, sure strokes, Lucy reached Charles. He threw his arms around her and held on for dear life.

"Let's get you out of here," she shouted.

"Oh God. Yes. Yes. I want to live. I want to speak at *his* funeral."

She began pulling him towards the shore. A smaller wave lifted them both and propelled them in the right direction. The riptide was less severe. Charles' feet could touch the ground.

"I came just as soon as you called."

"I celebrate you."

"I'm just glad I got here in time."

"I celebrate life."

"It's probably best to save your strength."

"I celebrate mankind."

"Seriously. Don't talk."

"I celebrate land."

He dropped to his knees and collapsed on the shore. They both remained there for several moments, catching their breath and bearings. Finally, Charles rolled over to his side, shook a little fish out of his sleeve, took Lucy's hand, and said, "You are an angel of mercy."

She smiled. This was hardly the beach scene of *From Here to Eternity*. Charles was no Burt Lancaster in a soaked business suit with kelp wrapped around his head and sand coming out of every orifice, and Lucy had blue lips, which Deborah Kerr did not, but as their eyes met there was that tiny *From Here to . . .* spark of electricity.

"Come on," she said sweetly. "Let's get that seaweed out of your ears."

****

He followed her to her apartment, which was not far away. Intermittent raindrops pinged off his windshield. Lucy lived in a modest one-bedroom rent-controlled apartment in Santa Monica. There were indoor plants everywhere, and they all seemed to be blooming. This girl injected life and vibrancy into everything she touched.

"There's the shower." She pointed. "And I think I have some old sweats you can wear."

"Your compassion frightens me," he said.

She smiled and gently pushed him into the bathroom. He closed the door, peeled off his wet, sticky, salty clothes, and stepped into the shower. He stood under the hot water—eyes closed—and relished the warmth and engulfing steam. At some point he would have to go home and try to patch things up with Sondra, but for the moment he was quite content to just give himself over to the pulsing water.

"Mind some company?"

He opened his eyes to see Lucy—naked, willowy, spectacular— join him in the shower. Noticing how aroused he instantly became, she added, "I didn't think so."

She pressed her lips and body against his.

The patching up of his marriage might have to wait a few minutes longer while he fucked another woman.

They did it in the shower. And then again on her bed. His spirits soared while making love. Was this so good because of his feelings towards Lucy? Or just the release he so desperately needed? Or the delicious irony that it was Stevie Gersh's girl? In any event, he was delirious with joy—*during*.

After—he was almost paralyzed. His troubles, fears, guilt, anger, and confusion all came roaring back with the force of an avalanche, and he began to shake.

Lucy held him tight.

"It's going to be all right," she assured him.

"No, it's not. I lost everything . . . including my moral compass. What do I do?! I called you, dear Lucy, because in this whole ugly world, you are the one person who's good, who's pure."

She squeezed him tight and beamed.

"I know what you can do, Charles," she purred.

He kissed her neck. "Ooh, I knew you would. I *knew* you would. What is it? Tell me. Anything. Anything!"

She reached into the nightstand drawer and pulled out a handgun.

"Kill him. Kill Stevie Gersh."

"Huh? What?" Charles was not expecting this.

Lucy spoke softly and lovingly. "Can't you see he has ruined both of our lives? The humiliation you feel is nothing compared to what he has done to me, to my reputation. Do you know what it's like for my sick mother—who was addicted to those gosh-darned tabloids before she was ill—to pick them up and see that I'm being called a whore in one, frigid in another, a scheming opportunist in this one, a foul-mouthed bitch in that one. It has got to stop. He has no right to destroy people like that . . . just because he's funny on television."

This was not the ideal time for Charles to make monumental decisions. He was still very much in a fog. Thank God she didn't spring this on him *while* they were having sex. He would have agreed to shoot the pope. But as he listened to Lucy he thought to himself she would be very good at pitching a show. She was clear and very concise. And she made some excellent points.

"He's a monster," Charles agreed, trying to sort his thoughts out loud. "And I created him. Well, not *me*. But somebody when I wasn't looking." He scratched his chin. "I'd like to kill *that* person too. But this, Lucy . . ."

"I know, darling," she said soothingly. "And you've had such a rough day."

"I have. And I got no sleep last night."

"But sometimes that's a good thing."

"It is?"

"Yes. You shed your inhibitions and act upon impulse. You give yourself over to your subconscious. You let your *inner you* guide you."

Charles shook his head. "My *inner me* told me to kill myself. You really think that should be my go-to guy?"

She gently placed the revolver in his hand.

"Oh God."

"It will make the pain go away."

"I want the pain to go away."

She slid down his chest.

"Then kill him."

CHAPTER 22

IN EVERY CITY OTHER THAN Los Angeles, gated residential communities were designed to keep out burglars. In LA they were to keep out TV news crews and paparazzi. Thank God he lived in one, Charles thought, as he drove past the phalanx of news vans and popping flashbulbs through the gates to his home. If Charles could take one small comfort, it was that the rain had picked up and the media vultures were getting soaked. All the hard-bitten TV journalists named Britney, Sibila, Amber, and Serene were at a real disadvantage when their hair got wet.

He pulled up to his house around seven thirty. Perhaps he and Sondra could still work things through. He was certainly less angry at his wife's indiscretion than he had been before his stop-off in Santa Monica.

But reconciliation was not to be.

By the time he had arrived, Sondra was already packed. She had nothing more to say than that some technicians from ABN had showed up needing something and she had let them in.

Charles hurried to his office to find them dismantling his multi-TV media center.

He next ducked into Kelly Rose's room, but she wasn't there. He heard the front door slam and rushed to the window.

In the now driving rain Sondra carried his daughter and a suitcase to her Lexus SUV. He watched forlornly as the climax of his family life played out. Before getting into the car, Kelly Rose looked up at her father sadly and waved good-bye. It was one of those touching moments right before a commercial break.

Charles was not a heavy-drinking man per se. He often negotiated great deals at lunch by nursing one drink while the agent/studio/manager across from him downed four. But this warranted a good stiff one. The only thing left to *negotiate* was whether he was going to carry out Lucy's lethal request. He took the revolver out of his jacket pocket and placed it in a drawer under the bar. Then he poured himself five fingers of Maker's Mark and drained it. Maybe this would make the pain go away without having to take a life. The stiff drink hit him like a Taser. He dropped to his hands and knees.

"Nope. I still feel the pain. And now I have the whirlies."

He rolled over and remained on the ground, waiting for the ceiling lights to stop spinning.

Half an hour must've passed. He could hear the technicians hauling the media center out of the house piece by piece. Eventually the door closed and that was that.

Once when Charles was a child his mother punished him for talking back to her (he had yelled, "You're a disgrace to Carol Brady!") and she took the TV out of his room for a week. This almost traumatized the young lad. No television for a week was like no food for a week, only worse because he missed a very special episode of *ALF*. His room felt empty without his nineteen-inch portable Sony. So empty he couldn't bear to be in it; the loss was just too great. Now *all* of his TVs were gone. And they weren't coming back in a week. Charles had been a *really* bad boy.

He replayed the encounter with Lucy in his mind. She had been so persuasive—to the point where he actually agreed to her proposal. But that was during the blow job. Afterwards he rescinded. But if anyone on the planet deserved not to live, it was Stevie Gersh. Not only was he a despicable human being who poisoned everything around him; he was rewarded and beloved for his efforts. Whatever happened to that little thing called *karma*? Charles could list a thousand reasons why he should kill him. *Ten* thousand. And yet, that still wasn't enough. Not to commit cold-blooded murder. But he was close. Teetering. Right on the very edge.

Loud, echoing chimes from the doorbell snapped him out of his reverie. Who the hell could that be? The front-gate security guards had strict instructions not to let anyone in.

Charles slowly got to his feet and staggered to the entrance hall on jelly legs. His head still felt like Sondra's SUV had backed over it.

He swung open the front door to find Detectives Staley and Long. They were both huddled under one umbrella, so both were getting drenched.

"Evening, Mr. Muncie. I'm detective Daniel Staley and this is Robbie—"

"Yes, I know who you are. I saw you six hours ago."

"Mind if we come in?"

"No. Of course." Charles ushered them into the house. What the fuck did *they* want?

"Thanks," said Detective Staley. "Lots of TV news crews out there."

"I'm aware."

"Wouldn't you love to see—just once—they go to the reporter live and he says, 'Well, I'm a mile from the house, that's as close as I'm ever going to get, and I don't know shit. No one's going to *tell* me shit. So I'll just camp out here for ten more hours and then report live that I still don't know shit'?"

"Back to you in the studio, Colleen," from his partner.

"Yes, that would be an uproarious scenario, but what do you need?"

"Y'know, it just occurred to me," said Staley, snapping his fingers. "This would make a great, very cinematic scene for that show we're proposing. Two detectives standing in the rain. The job can get messy sometimes. But that's what makes it *real*."

"You came to my home, my sanctuary, during the dinner hour to pitch your show again?"

"No, but two birds. Okay, this is a stretch, but imagine if you saw us and decided to run. Can you picture that chase scene? In the driving rain. Close on our feet: Splish-splash, splish-splash with every step. Then the big takedown. Plop! Right into the mud. 'Oh no!

That's nasty!' America is saying. Maybe we roll around a little. Some mud clods spray the camera. It's authentic. That's what happens. You can't expect pretty shots every minute. Again, it's not something we've ever actually *done*, but it's always a possibility, and others have done it."

"You realize how inappropriate this is?"

"Don't worry. It's not the main reason we're here. You've become a prime suspect, but when whole action sequences just pop into your head, you know you're onto something good."

During the preceding the detectives had peeled off their yellow rain slickers with *LAPD* in block letters on the back.

"Kinda hard to go undercover wearing these things," said Detective Long. His partner chuckled. Charles did not.

"What do you mean I'm a suspect?" he asked. "I thought I answered all of your questions this afternoon. I was quite candid and forthright. And how did that damn diary go public? You assured me you were going to keep it confidential."

"Yeah, sorry about that. Turns out the guy who checks in evidence is the brother of one of the *TMZ* producers," Staley said.

"You wonder why we can't convict anybody," added Long.

"Well, that little slip cost me my position, destroyed my entire career!"

"Really? Oh, jeez. That's terrible. Again, our oops."

Long hung his slicker on a coat rack. "Although with all due respect, if you kept your dick in your pants . . ."

"And your lizard tongue in your mouth . . ."

Charles just grumbled. "Yeah, yeah."

"I guess there goes our series idea, huh?" lamented Long.

"Yeah. Shit."

"Who replaced you?" asked Staley.

"Do you mind?!" Charles replied.

"Just curious."

"Hey, we have a little bit of a stake in this now."

"I don't know who's replacing me."

"Come on, you must have some idea."

"What do you want?!" Charles pleaded in exasperation.

"Have you been drinking, Mr. Muncie?" said Staley, getting a good whiff of his breath.

"Yes. I'm in my own house. Is that a problem? Is there now a law against that? Has prohibition returned? Because if so, tell me, please. I need to get started on that reboot of *The Untouchables!*"

"No need to smack talk us, Mr. Muncie. We're just trying to assess your state of mind. Good detective work is not just asking questions and getting answers; it's evaluating said answers. Accuracy can be colored by emotion or a diminished capacity. It's up to us trained professionals, if you will, to sometimes read between the blurry lines. Damn! There's no detective show on television showing this," Staley said.

"I'm fine," Charles insisted.

"Would you happen to have a club soda?" Long asked.

"Yes, in the bar. Help yourself."

Detective Long thanked him and crossed to the bottles.

"Now, seriously," Charles said, "how can I possibly be a suspect? I told you I was at a charity dinner that night. There were a thousand witnesses who heard me speak. Surely some of them were awake and can vouch for me."

Detective Staley got out his trusty iPad mini and got down to business. "Well, our office received a call about an hour ago from a Mr. Stevie Gersh. That was quite a thrill, I don't have to tell you."

Holy shit! Gersh ratted him out? That motherfucker!

"What did he want?" Charles said, suddenly stone sober.

"Where's a bottle opener?" Long asked at the bar.

"In a drawer," Charles answered absentmindedly. And then it hit him. *The gun.* The gun was in one of the drawers.

"Wait!" Charles yelled. "Let me get it for you."

"That's really not necessary. I'll just find it."

Charles practically vaulted to the bar. "No. I keep everything in precise order. I'm very anal that way."

Long had no trouble buying that. Charles opened the gun drawer for one split second and produced the bottle opener.

"Thanks," said the detective, popping off the cap. He returned to the living room followed by his greatly relieved host. Not that he was out of hot water.

"Mr. Gersh claimed that you went over to his house today and confessed to murdering Anji DeVelera," said Detective Staley, referring to his iPad.

"That's so patently absurd it doesn't even warrant a response," Charles scoffed.

"Well, warrant one anyway."

"I want to have my lawyer present."

Detective Long cursed. "Aw, Christ. Mr. Muncie, we drove all the way out here. It's raining like a son of a bitch. Wilshire was a crawl. We don't have a siren. All the news vans clogging up the gate. If you're so damn innocent and have nothing to hide, just answer the goddamn questions."

"All right. First off—no, I did not murder Anji DeVelera. But in the spirit of full disclosure, I did, in fact, go to Stevie Gersh's house today where—even fuller disclosure—I caught him in bed with my wife."

"Ouch!"

"Yes. That sacred bond of marital trust that I cherish above all else was ruptured forever. I was subjected to the ultimate betrayal."

"Wow. This has not been a good day for you."

"Ya think? I tell you that not to garner any sympathy for me, but because (a) I am being truthful even at the expense of my own dignity, and (b) to illustrate that this is just another example of how Stevie Gersh has taken on a personal campaign to destroy me. Gentlemen, Stevie Gersh is not who you think he is. He is a spiteful, sick, hateful Visigoth whose single greatest delight in the world is hurting others."

Staley shook his head. "I find that a little hard to believe."

"Of course you do!" Charles shouted. "Everyone thinks of him as the fun-loving scamp he plays on TV, but that's bullshit! And you *trained professionals*, who can so acutely spot transparencies, should see that."

"He was nice on the phone." Staley shrugged.

"Google the name Lucy Adamson and see what you get. Article after article smearing this modern-day Madonna's good name. And why? Because she had the audacity to reject his proposal of marriage. Call up the *Gersh* one-hundredth-episode party on YouTube and watch him sit me in a fucking cake."

"Seen it. Must've been six people emailed me that link."

"Cruelty is the oxygen that this Mothra breathes!"

Long took a swig of his club soda. "Well, why does he have it so in for you, Mr. Muncie?"

"Because his contract is up and negotiations have been very contentious. Because I'm the one man who will stand up to his tyranny. I'm the one man who will tell him no! And he wants me out of the way . . . especially now that he's schtupping the mother of my child. Although, I have to admit, even *I* didn't think he would stoop so low as to frame me for a murder. My God! Actors!"

Neither detective said anything. Staley just took down notes.

"I can assure you—Stevie Gersh has many enemies," Charles continued. "Were something sinister to hypothetically happen to him and you did get that show of yours on the air, you could spend the entire first season sifting through the suspects."

"We'd prefer stand-alone episodes, I think."

"Focus. You're missing the point."

"No. We hear ya. He's got a lot of haters."

"What reason did Stevie give for why I allegedly killed Ms. De-Velera?" Charles asked.

"To entice him to do his show another couple of years."

"By killing somebody," Charles said. "That's how Global United Industries, a major conglomerate that's ranked nineteenth on the S&P 500 and accountable to shareholders and the SEC, does routine business—by murdering people when negotiations hit a snag. Gentlemen, just listen to how preposterous that sounds, even for Wall Street."

Staley shrugged and admitted that as motives go, that wasn't the strongest.

"And why would I kill Anji DeVelera to please Stevie Gersh?" Charles was starting to feel better. His ability to talk his way through sticky situations was slowly returning. "What connection was there between her and Gersh? He only met her the day before. Was Stevie's name even mentioned in her diary?"

"No, actually."

"Then what he's claiming is that in order to get him to continue his television series I killed a casual acquaintance. Yes, that's the first step they teach you at Wharton business school." Maybe Charles could get an assignment writing a legal drama. That was a pretty slick cross-examination. He made a mental note to call *The Good Wife* or that one on USA about the babe lawyer with the big tits.

Detective Staley powered down his iPad mini.

"Well, you make some good points, Mr. Muncie."

Charles was feeling his oats. "Have him come down and sign a statement. Get it on the record. Then when you find the real killer, I can sue him for every last cent he owns. And that, gentlemen, is how a *civilized* man ruins some cocksucker's life."

The detectives thanked him, uttered the standard "sorry to bother you so late" tropes while donning their slickers, and started to leave when Long turned back.

"Oh, one more thing."

Charles rolled his eyes. "Really? Another '*Columbo* moment'? Now?"

"No," Detective Long said. "I've still got this." He held up the bottle opener.

"Oh. Sorry. Thank you. I'll put it away."

Long handed it to him, they bid Charles good night again, and they were just about out the door when Staley turned back.

"If you weren't there to confess to Ms. DeVelera's murder, then why did you go visit Mr. Gersh today?"

A curveball, but he could handle it.

"To offer him a private jet if he agreed to resume his series." *Nicely done,* he thought.

"A private jet? And he hated you why?"

"I told you. I'm the one person who doesn't coddle him."

"Yeah, you must've really put him in his place with that private jet offer."

"It's complicated."

"He wanted two private jets?"

"There's a thing called gamesmanship, gentlemen. Knowing what to say, playing the other person to get him to do or believe what you want him to do or believe. The plane was a bargaining chip. And it came with many very stiff demands, none of which I'm at liberty to discuss right now."

Staley arched an eyebrow. "You're good at that, Mr. Muncie? Getting people to believe what you want them to?"

Charles realized his gaffe. "That's not what I meant. I was being one hundred percent truthful with you. But that's real life. This is Hollywood. No one tells the truth when negotiating in Hollywood. You'd wind up homeless in the streets owning only the Israeli foreign rights to the next Mel Gibson picture."

"Well, I hope you're telling the truth," said Detective Long, popping open the wet umbrella. "Because the eyes of the world are watching and we're going to solve this case. That's a news bulletin you can quote me on."

And to punctuate that official statement, his partner added, "Back to you in the studio, Colleen."

This time they did leave, and Charles locked the door behind them. Goddamn "*Columbo* moments"!

But one positive thing did come out of this interrogation. By reporting him to the police, Stevie had given Charles that one final reason.

He crossed to the bar, opened the drawer, returned the bottle opener, and removed the gun.

CHAPTER 23

HE NEEDED AN ALIBI. If he was going to do this, he had to be shrewd. He went upstairs to his office, ignored the gaping hole that once was his beloved media center, and thumbed through the stacks of scripts on his shelves, hoping to jog his memory. Surely there was a great murder scheme in a pilot that ultimately didn't sell or a high-quality but low-rated cop show he canceled three airings in. After twenty minutes of perusing medical pilots, antiterrorism pilots, *Game of Thrones* clones, and legal thrillers—*eureka*! In the never-broadcast *Blood Lines* starring Sharon and Kelly Osbourne as a mother-daughter detective team, there was the trumped-up alibi he was looking for. Plotting was definitely not the problem with *that* project.

With the storm continuing to rage, Charles drove quickly past the vigilant news vans to the Nuart Theatre on Santa Monica Boulevard in West Los Angeles. The ornate Nuart was one of the last remaining revival theaters—a *sanctuary* for old movies. Video rentals and Netflix had effectively killed these odes to a simpler time. Lost, of course, was the joy of experiencing these classic motion pictures in their intended form—on a big screen with an audience texting.

Charles parked on a side street, and even if he had to walk half a block in a monsoon, it was worth it. He needed the Jaguar to be unseen when he left.

The double bill that night was *The Big Sleep* and *The Maltese Falcon*, two movies that Charles had seen so could easily discuss should anyone ask, although nobody could recite the plot of *The Big Sleep*, so that one was a gimme.

First stop was the 7-Eleven across the street. He bought a large bag of M&M'S. Even though it was one item, he paid by credit card. And he stood right in front of the store's security camera when he made the transaction. There was now a paper trail and video proof that he'd been there. Also important: He was seen sopping wet.

Charles crossed the street to the theater and paid for his admission with a credit card. The paper trail continued. Charles asked the tatted high school girl in the box office if any Phoebe Cates movies were on the upcoming schedule (a longtime crush since *Fast Times at Ridgemont High*). He wanted to be memorable should anyone in a day or two ask if she had seen him. Tat girl had never heard of Phoebe Cates, so she just said no.

Charles found a seat just as *The Big Sleep* was starting. The entire double bill, he calculated, would last at least four hours. How plausible that he would wish to hide from the media throng in a darkened movie theater. This was the perfect alibi.

He stayed through the first scene, then slipped out the side exit and returned to his car. Next stop: Malibu.

****

This was a three-mile-per-hour night on Pacific Coast Highway. Mudslides were everywhere. Charles had plenty of time to reconsider. But his mind was made up. Did President Obama have reservations about killing Osama bin Laden? Not a chance. He probably wished he could have pulled the trigger. Imagine what a campaign spot that would have been. "I'm Barack Obama and I approve this message." *Blammo!*

But there was still plenty of time to do the dirty deed and scamper back to the Nuart before Bogie told Mary Astor she had to "take the fall."

Listening to the radio for company, Charles heard this on the National Public Radio station, KCRW: "And in show business news, ABN president Charles Muncie was fired today. And Stevie Gersh announced that he will continue his show for another three years.

KEN LEVINE | 145

Makes you wonder if somehow the two events weren't related."

Normally a public pantsing like that would be a dagger to Charles' heart, but on this night it merely strengthened his resolve. His steely look of determination was downright frightening. Think Nicholson in *The Shining.*

He parked the Jaguar a house away from his prey's. Charles was being extracareful. *Pretty impressive for a non-pro assassin,* he thought as he dropped a few rounds into the chamber. He engaged the safety, tucked the weapon inside his jacket, and trudged over to Stevie's palatial beach cottage. The rain continued to pelt him, but he didn't hurry. He was a man of singular purpose.

He reached Stevie's front door and without hesitation rang the bell. He stood patiently in the downpour waiting for a response. When one was not forthcoming after a minute, he rang the bell again, this time keeping his finger pressed on the button.

"Who is it?" a groggy Stevie Gersh called out on the squawk box.

"Charles Muncie. Let me in."

There was a pause.

"Can't do that, Charlie."

"Open the door, please."

"It's very late."

"Open the door."

"Your wife's not here."

"Open. The. Door."

"Look, Charles. From now on if you want to communicate with me, you call my legal team."

Charles pulled his gun out, carefully removed the safety, stood back, and blasted the doorknob off.

"What the fuck?!" was heard on the squawk box.

Charles kicked the door open and calmly entered. With both hands he trained the revolver on Stevie.

"Hi. It's the network."

CHAPTER 24

STEVIE INSTANTLY PANICKED. He began backing away. Charles advanced step for step, keeping his target in the crosshairs.

"Oh shit. Easy. Easy," said Stevie. "Look, what happened, happened. I didn't plan it. I wasn't out to bust up anybody's marriage. And as far as the police—they came to *me*, dude. They pressured me to make that statement. I didn't want to do it. I mean, I had no proof. You could have just been bullshitting me. How did I know? But they were relentless. And mean. They broke me. I'm weak. Okay? I told them what you said. But it wasn't my idea. I had to."

"Shut the fuck up."

"I can go on Jimmy Kimmel and say I was coerced."

"Did you hear me? I said shut up!"

They were both in the middle of the room now. Stevie was almost ready to wet himself.

"Look, man," he pleaded. "What do you want? Anything. Anything at all. I mean, *anything*."

His tormenter smiled wryly. "Ironic, isn't it? Now you're the one begging."

"Is that it? You want me to beg?"

Stevie fell to his knees, his hands clasped together. "Money? The house? A piece of the show? With the extra three years we could be talking, like, for you, twenty . . . thirty million dollars."

Charles fired off a warning shot into the ceiling.

Stevie screamed and blurted out, "Eighty million!"

Charles returned the gun to Stevie. "I bet you regret calling your fortune 'fuck *God money*' now, huh? I don't want your riches. Can't you understand? I just want you dead. *Dead!*"

He put the gun to Stevie's head. Stevie dissolved into tears.

Charles stood over him for a long moment, just watching him wail. At first he savored the sight. This was what he'd dreamed about every single day for four years. The only thing better would have been if Stevie were sitting in a cake. Who knew all it would take was a firearm?

Charles debated over whether to whip out his iPhone and capture this touching little performance on video. How fast would *that* go viral on YouTube? Forget YouTube; it should have its own Web site. Charles had the title, too. *Funny AND Die.* But of course hit man Charles Muncie was too savvy to do anything that would incriminate himself, so he would just have to be content with the mental picture of TV's biggest star reduced to a blubbering, pathetic wretch.

But Charles was finding it hard to pull the trigger. He wanted to pull the trigger. He wanted to in the worst way. And yet . . .

He just stood there, the weapon quivering in his hands. "Goddamn, I'm gonna do it . . . I'm gonna do it," he said through gritted teeth, trying to will his finger to squeeze the trigger.

Stevie looked up. Was there a chance? Would he be spared?

Frustrated, Charles lowered the gun.

"Oh, thank God!" Stevie sighed with relief.

Charles returned the gun to his head.

"Shut up! I'm just taking a break. I'm still going to do it."

More agonizing seconds ticked away, sweat and tears pouring out of Stevie Gersh.

So many clashing ideas were shouting over one another in Charles' head. He let out a guttural yell, as if that might silence them and help him pull the damn trigger.

Stevie screamed in terror.

"Shut up!" Charles yelled and blasted another shot into the ceiling.

Again he held the pistol against Stevie's temple. He closed his eyes tight and turned away. *Now! Now! Do it now!*

But he couldn't.

He just couldn't.

Charles lowered the gun.

He turned to go, paused, then turned back.

"Fuck you! You son of a bitch! I'm Charles Muncie," he said with pride. "I was the entertainment president of ABN. I took them to number one. I'm Charles Muncie! Charles fucking Muncie! I'm not going to let you destroy me like this. You can't because I'm better than you! You fucking heathen! My mother, on her deathbed, said to me, success isn't measured by how much you make; it's measured by how much you give. I'm giving you your miserable life, Stevie. And that makes me a success."

Stevie remained a heap on the floor.

"Thank you, Charles. Thank you . . . I celebrate you," he whimpered.

"What?! Are you mocking me?"

"Huh? No. I'm sorry. I thought it's what you would have liked to hear. I don't know what to say after a speech like that. Jesus!"

Charles let it pass. He had other items on his agenda.

"Now. This little affair you're having with my wife . . ."

"Oh man, that is so over."

"And that fucking statement you made to the police . . ."

"I am calling first thing in the morning to clear that up. It was a mistake. I misheard."

"Good. Because if you don't . . ."

"I will, I will. Believe me."

"If you don't I'm coming back. I will blow your shit away, so help me God, and then I'll go to the Reel Inn and have a lovely meal. It might even be Copper River salmon season again."

"I'll do it. I'll do it. I swear."

"If I hear they have Copper River salmon I may kill you anyway. It's silly to drive all this way just for one thing."

"Please. I'll call. I'll end it with Sondra. I'll go back to Lucy."

"You won't go back to Lucy!" Charles roared, raising the gun again.

"I won't go back to Lucy," Stevie repeated immediately. "No Lucy. No Sondra, no Lucy, no Lana—"

"Lana?! You fucked my assistant, Lana?"

"Okay . . . I'm just really going to shut up now."

Charles shook his head. He had raised the gun this time to scare him, but Jesus, if he hadn't just delivered that lofty speech, he damn well might have pulled the trigger. Four times.

He shifted the focus back to Lucy. "Within forty-eight hours I expect to see a retraction in every tabloid and gossip show for the fallacious, spiteful things you said about Lucy Adamson."

"What does fallacious mean?"

"I swear! Don't mock me!"

"No. Seriously. No one uses those words."

"Okay. Say your fucking prayers . . ."

"No! Wait! I'll clear things with Lucy. I'll call the tabloids. I'll put up a billboard. I'll buy a dictionary. Whatever. You got it."

Charles Muncie stood over the disheveled man he had just broken.

"Stevie Gersh . . . ?" he said.

"Yes?" Stevie answered weakly.

"You have lost a viewer."

And with that Charles lowered the gun, returned the safety, and triumphantly marched out.

The heavy rain came down in a slant now. Charles slogged head-first into it. He didn't mind. The rain felt cleansing and invigorating. Sparing Stevie Gersh was something he would have to live with for the rest of his life, but he felt that with time, faith, therapy, alcohol, and Lucy, he could.

The gun was still in his hand as he trudged along Pacific Coast Highway.

His mind was racing with a cacophony of thoughts. How often is a man faced with a major ethical decision? Did Lucy keep a personal diary? Shooting that gun was cool; he could see what enthusiasts saw in it. Stevie fucked Lana? How safe was this rainwater to drink? Was his inability to kill Stevie a sign of strength or weakness?

Was he better in the sack than Stevie? Was a show about real-life detectives worth pursuing? Can you really get cancer from cunnilingus? And then . . . a brainstorm.

With a devilish smile, he turned back. He fought his way to the side of Stevie's house and carefully clip-clopped down the slippery wooden steps to the beach.

Would Stevie make good on his promises? Probably not. If he squared things with the police and cleared Lucy's sullied name, that would suffice. Sleeping with Sondra seemed less of an issue at this point. Maybe they deserved each other. And let's see how Stevie liked it when she kicked him out of bed for checking the Tuesday overnights.

Screwing Lana irked him a little bit, though. He secretly always wanted to sleep with Lana but felt it would have been grossly inappropriate. Besides, who knew if she even had feelings for him? Charles cursed himself. He at least should have shot off Stevie's dick.

But he knew now that he would never use the gun. So he gazed out at the angry sea and flung the weapon far into the night. It pinwheeled over the eroding beach and landed in the drink with a resounding splash. Considering the tide, within an hour it would wash up onto the shore either in front of David Geffen's house or in China.

Now to the real order of business: Charles couldn't kill Stevie, but at least he could exact some sweet revenge.

He grabbed one of the sandbags pressed up against the terrace to buttress it. He flipped the heavy bag over and began pouring out the sand.

One down; twenty-six more to go.

CHAPTER 25

STEVIE GERSH REMAINED in shock, cowering on the floor, for at least ten minutes. Eventually he got to his vibrating knees and slowly rose to his wobbly feet. He took a couple of deep breaths. His hands could not stop shaking. Rain was still gushing in from the open front door, saturating and staining the plush white carpeting and matching custom-made Italian designer furniture. But he ignored that. Instead he crossed to the bar and poured himself the stiffest drink he ever had in his life.

He took a couple of swigs, then let out a monumental sigh of relief.

Barely heard over the tempest was a short, muffled sound.

Stevie pitched forward and landed face-first on the floor.

Dead.

From out of the shadows, Robert McManus, the hit man, emerged. He strolled over to the body and kicked it. Once satisfied that there was no more life in it, he kicked it again. The second kick was because he had overheard the recent confrontation with Charles and knew he deserved it. Robert then produced a disposable cell phone out of his pocket and dialed a number.

When the other party answered, he said, "It's done."

Marc Jantzen, working late in his spacious office at Fox, was on his own disposable cell phone.

"Fine . . . We'll talk. By the way, I liked the Civil War idea."

Marc hung up, smiled broadly, sauntered over to the big magnetic display board, and said with a wry chuckle, "Well, that kind of frees up Tuesday night."

****

In the dark, under Stevie Gersh's house, a shadowy figure worked like a dervish, whistling a happy tune. Charles held his ground against the ferocious winds and driving rain while emptying sandbags. There *was* something calming about the beach, he thought as his hair stuck out like Don King's. Too bad he had to scurry back to the Nuart so soon. He'd once approached Barbra Streisand about doing a comeback special on ABN and she wouldn't even talk to him. He'd love to go over and pour out her sandbags too.

Suddenly, his face was hit with a blinding light.

"Hey, buddy, what're you doin' out here?" from a voice behind the flashlight.

Charles squinted to see who was talking. The flashlight belonged to two uniformed policemen in now-familiar yellow slickers who were patrolling the beach.

"Oh, good evening, Officers. I was just helping with the sandbags," Charles lied cheerfully.

The cop not holding the light said, "Looks like you're emptying them."

"Yeah . . . well, he wants them moved, and they're easier to move . . . when the bags are empty." This was the last thing Charles needed.

"A neighbor called and reported hearing gunshots."

Thank God he had disposed of the gun. Hopefully it wouldn't wash up at his feet.

"I heard thunder. I suspect that is what the homeowner heard," he answered. He was wily, that Charles.

The other cop pointed the beam and said, "Isn't this Stevie Gersh's house? That's where she heard the shots fired."

"Yeah, I think it is," said his partner, who then turned to Charles. "Step away from the bags, sir."

"Gentlemen, this is silly."

"Drop the bag. I mean it."

"And put your hands where we can see them."

Charles did and held up his hands. The flashlight cop asked who he was.

"I know Mr. Gersh. I'm Charles Muncie. You've probably seen me on all the news channels tonight."

"Why would you be on the news?"

That was dumb. He was going to tell them it was because he was a suspect in a murder case? That would really assuage any suspicion. Instead, he said, "I won the lottery. But I do know Stevie Gersh."

"Is that right?"

"Yes. We've known each other for years."

The cop nodded and aimed the beam at the wooden staircase that led from the beach to the street. "All right. Well, let's go find out from Mr. Gersh."

"Fine," said Charles, inwardly kicking himself for not just leaving when he had the chance. Oh well. This would be awkward but would only take another five minutes. He'd soon be on his way.

****

Sondra was too stunned to cry. She sat in her hotel room in the Beverly Hilton absolutely slack jawed over the unimaginable images parading across her television. Shots of her husband being loaded into a police car. Shots of the covered body of Stevie Gersh being removed from a blood-soaked room she herself had been in only hours before. And the words from the news anchor were nothing short of surreal.

"More developments in the shocking death of comedian superstar Stevie Gersh. Police have arrested former ABN network president, Charles Muncie, who was found skulking around Gersh's Malibu beachfront home earlier in the evening. We spoke to detectives Daniel Staley and Robbie Long, who are heading this investigation."

Staley and Long would have their real-life detective TV show after all.

They stood before the camera. Staley spoke first.

"We have motive and the opportunity. And yes, Mr. Muncie, we believe, is responsible for the death of Mr. Gersh."

"He does have an alibi," his partner chimed in, "but it doesn't hold up. Actually, he used a gambit that had been seen just last week on *Castle*."

"Not to mention an episode of *Law and Order* and *Starsky and Hutch*."

"And *Kojak*."

"It was used twice on *Kojak*."

"Right. And I think *Simon and Simon*."

"In any event, we are also looking at him for a possible connection in the Anji DeVelera murder."

CHAPTER 26

THE TRIAL WAS A TELEVISION sensation. Among eighteen- to thirty-four-year-olds it outranked the O.J. Simpson trial. Charles trended higher on Twitter than Justin Bieber for four whole weeks. The *Muncie Murders* late-night daily wrap-up show hosted by Ryan Seacrest on ABN crushed Dave and all the Jimmys. Guest legal experts included former attorney/writer David E. Kelley, and Robert and Michelle King, the creators of *The Good Wife*. Sondra and Kelly Rose fled to the south of France to avoid the constant cameras. Charles' loyal assistant, Lana, proved to be so good in her sound bytes that she wound up a judge on *America's Got Talent*. Detective Staley used his notoriety to fund a movie from Kickstarter that he starred in along with Ann Curry. Sandbag sales went up dramatically.

Anji got a star on the Hollywood Walk of Fame. Elton John added lyrics to "Candle in the Wind" and hit the charts for the first time in fifteen years. Her caricature went up in the Palm. It was placed in the coveted spot between Natalie Wood and the creator of *Mad Men*.

The new direction of *Blue Justice* finally started to catch on. In fact, after Neil Patrick Harris guested as the singing serial killer, it became a breakout hit, which is practically impossible five years into a series' run. By November it was the top-rated show of the year. Even without *Gersh*, those numbers would have saved Charles' job and allowed him to coast for another three years.

Meanwhile, his entire life was dissected on television. Programming decisions he had made three years ago were debated on *Hannity*. Anji DeVelera's diary outsold *Fifty Shades of Grey* and was optioned by Jerry Bruckheimer for a major motion picture starring Katherine Heigl and Ryan Gosling (as Charles). *20/20* retraced the night Charles' mom slept with Ted Turner. Judd Apatow optioned that incident for a TV movie starring Leslie Mann. The Courtyard by Marriott became San Bernardino's number one tourist attraction, eclipsing even the first McDonald's. A one-man off-Broadway show called *Celebrating Charles* was packing 'em in with Steve Buscemi playing Charles. A book came out claiming that CBS founder William S. Paley had Rod Serling murdered. Another book speculated that programming czar Fred Silverman was responsible for the untimely demise of *Hogan's Heroes'* Bob Crane.

Stevie's house was turned into a shrine. He was awarded an Emmy posthumously. His five-year-old comedy album won a Grammy. He replaced Charles as the B'nai B'rith Humanitarian of the Year. Stevie Gersh impersonators began popping up all over the country. A one-man off-Broadway show called *Too Soon?* was turning people away with Zach Braff starring as Stevie. Two streets in New York were named in his honor. Cocktail waitresses at Caesars Palace, where he used to perform, wore black ankle garters for a month. Every network carried the funeral live. Fox had a red carpet show. TBS did a split screen—the memorial service on the left and best episodes of his show on the right. Delivering the eulogy, Tracy Morgan proclaimed him a comic genius, joining the ranks of Woody Allen, Mel Brooks, Lucille Ball, and him. Jay Leno bought all his cars. The Screen Actors Guild established a hotline for actors to report abusive corporate management. Former American Idol Taylor Hicks had his first number one hit with his cover of "Abraham, Martin, and Stevie."

Sondra completely cut herself off from the world. That was the only way she could avoid all the hoopla and shield her daughter from any of it. She stayed off the Internet, granted no interviews, and refused to meet with Teri Hatcher, who was signed to play her in the movie.

She didn't even watch the verdict live. Like everyone else in the world, she knew what it was going to be. Nor did she watch the sentencing live (which got higher numbers than even the *Friends* finale).

When she finally broke down and caught CNN International that night, she gasped upon seeing her husband. Charles was now completely gray. He was drawn and thin and had aged two presidential terms in less than a year. Tears filled her eyes as the anchor filed his report.

"Charles Muncie was sentenced today to life in prison for the murder of the beloved comic Stevie Gersh. Muncie, once known as the golden boy of network television, will serve his sentence at the state penitentiary in Chino, California. We don't know what work he'll eventually be assigned to do there, but I doubt if it will be network president."

Sondra turned off the television. In Charles Muncie's worldview, turning off the television was the ultimate rejection.

Two days later Charles was transferred to Chino. By now he was in an almost permanent state of numbness. He was processed in, told to change into the orange jumpsuit he would be wearing every day for God knew how many years, issued his bedding, and escorted into his cell block by a burly guard.

It was larger and louder and brighter and far more ominous than he had imagined from watching prison series on TV. He thought back to *David Cassidy: Man Undercover*, a late seventies NBC series in which teen heartthrob Cassidy played a cop who each week went undercover for a different case. In one episode he went undercover in a maximum-security prison. This was just a few years after *The Partridge Family*. Looking around this cell block and the animals in these cages, Charles almost had to chuckle. Pretty boy David Cassidy would last eleven seconds in here. He would be a Snickers bar in a fat farm.

Better to think about the implausibility of a bogus TV show than listen to the taunts from the real convicts who were his new neighbors. One by one they shouted as he passed by.

"Hey! It's the network president!"

"Ooh yeah . . . fresh meat!"

"I hate all your shows!"

"You killed Gersh! You are fucking dead!"

Prison Break on Fox was more realistic but still stretched credibility, Charles thought. You could give Wentworth Miller all the tattoos you wanted, but with that sweet face? The line to get at him would be so long you'd think they were giving away free iPhones. Prisoners would waive early release to get to him.

"You're mine, sweet thing!"

"Hey! Put *this* on your network!"

"Can you get me a date with Katherine Heigl?"

Singing: "Can anybody here see my old friend Stevie?"

They arrived at his dismal, claustrophobic cell—a bed, toilet, empty shelf for his meager belongings. *Oz* was right on the money with its depiction of a prison cell.

Charles stepped inside and a loud clang echoed as the heavy steel door was shut behind him.

How would this change him? he wondered. Charles now had plenty of time for his flights of fancy. How bitter would he become? Did they miss a bet not making *Oz* a woman's prison? *Orange Is the New Black* was a smash on Netflix. Women were the new men. What about all-women coal miners? Was there even such a thing? Whom should he stay in touch with? How often would he need to clean the toilet? He assumed the prison didn't provide maid service. Who actually did kill Stevie? And why? How did his cell compare to Phil Spector's? Why hadn't he just gotten in the car and gone back to the Nuart that fateful night? What tattoos to get? Was he the highest-ranking television executive ever to be incarcerated? How would ABN fill the late night now that the trial was over? If they were smart it would be an all-women something. In six months would David Cassidy start to look good to him, too?

****

Those first six months passed.

Charles was led into the visitor's room, where Lucy Adamson was waiting for him. He sat across the glass from her and picked up the phone. She looked as lovely as ever in a white blouse and blue skirt. He looked less grim. He had a gang tattoo on one arm and a small *ALF* on his neck.

"Charles, good news!" Lucy said after exchanging pleasantries. "I spoke to my attorney. There may be a way that we can reopen this case."

Charles smiled at the gesture. "Lucy, I appreciate that, but please. That's not necessary. I don't want to reopen the case."

"Why? I don't understand. You want to spend your life in jail?"

"I'm guilty of some things, but more than that . . . yes, I like it here."

"What?" Lucy was beyond shocked.

Charles leaned in. "At first, it was an absolute nightmare. Alone, in a tiny cell. Torn away from society and the life I loved. Forced to join a gang for protection. The one I chose is very tolerable if you just ignore all the 'Third Reich will rise again' rhetoric."

"But early on, I found a book to pass the time. It had been so long since I just read a book. It was wonderful. Glorious. Liberating. And I began to read more. And of course, I had all the time in the world to savor and celebrate every one. It became my passion. Sitting in my little cell, I realized there's a whole world out there. A world of imagination. My imagination. If I perform a certain, uh . . . *nicety* on one of the guys, he's going to get me a Kindle. But you can't believe how thrilling it is to read for pleasure and not option. I don't know if you can see it, but I think some blond hair is beginning to grow back in."

The excitement in his voice was palpable. "And I've begun to write. There's this children's book I'm noodling with that I want to dedicate to Kelly Rose. One of the fellas in the gang is doing the illustrations. We'll have to airbrush out the swastikas, but the bunnies he draws are adorable."

Lucy didn't know what to think. "You're serious? You're happy?"

Charles was practically beaming. "Oh sure, there's a downside. The food is hellacious. And I'm going to have to pick a daddy soon or they'll pick one for me. But hey, it's a small price to pay to be out of television."

THE END

Acknowledgements:

The core of this novel stems from an unsold screenplay I wrote along with David Isaacs. So thanks to David for some of the best things in the book.

Lee Goldberg is my publishing and novel writing guru. People always say they couldn't have done it without so-and-so, but in this case it's really true.

Several established authors were extremely generous with their time and advice. Enormous thanks to Tom Straw and Beth Ciotta.

Eileen Chetti dotted the I's and crossed the T's after I had crossed the I's and dotted the T's. Her copyediting was invaluable.

Jeroen ten berge creates the best covers in the business. And a nod to Jason Chatraw of Green E-Books for his formatting.

Special thanks to some special friends – Blair Richwood, Richard & Sara Rosenstock, Phoef Sutton, Howard Hoffman, Jonathan Emerson, and Kevin Gershan.

And finally, immeasurable gratitude to my family for their love and support. My wife, Debby, son, Matthew, and daughter, Annie somehow put up with all my craziness, which is the same whether I'm writing a book or not.

About the Author:

KEN LEVINE is an Emmy winning writer/director/producer/ major league baseball announcer. In a career that has spanned over 30 years Ken has worked on *MASH*, *Cheers*, *Frasier*, *The Simpsons*, *Wings*, *Everybody Loves Raymond*, *Becker*, *Dharma & Greg*, and has co-created his own series including *Almost Perfect* starring Nancy Travis. He and his partner wrote the feature *Volunteers* starring Tom Hanks and John Candy.

Ken has also been the radio/TV play-by-play voice of the Baltimore Orioles, Seattle Mariners, and San Diego Padres, and has hosted pre-and-postgame shows for the Los Angeles Dodgers.

Ken is the author of three other books. His memoir, *The Me Generation…By Me (Growing Up in the '60s)*, and a compilation of his humorous travelogues, *Where the Hell Am I? Trips I Have Survived* are both available in ebook and paperback form on Amazon.com.

He also wrote a chronicle of his year sportscasting in Baltimore, entitled *It's Gone…No, Wait A Minute*, published by Villard in 1993,

His blog, byKenLevine.com was named "One of the Top 25 Blogs on the Internet" by *Time* Magazine.

Made in the USA
San Bernardino, CA
05 January 2014